VIOLIN EXERCISES FOR KIDS

Engaging activities to
help children learn and
enjoy playing the violin

Francesca Jackson

DEDICATION

This book is dedicated to all the young
violinists whose passion for music
inspires them to learn and grow.

TABLE OF CONTENTS

INTRODUCTION TO VIOLIN EXERCISES FOR CHILDREN

The violin is a beautiful and versatile musical instrument that has captured the hearts of people for centuries. Introducing children to the world of violin playing can be a rewarding and enriching experience. Violin exercises designed specifically for children help them develop essential skills, foster creativity, and instill a lifelong passion for music.

1. The Joy of Learning the Violin

- Exploring the melodious sound of the violin

- Cultivating a sense of accomplishment through progress

- Developing a love for music and self-expression

2. Benefits of Violin Exercises for Children

- Enhancing cognitive abilities such as memory and concentration

- Improving fine motor skills and hand-eye coordination

- Boosting creativity, self-discipline, and patience

- Providing an avenue for emotional expression and stress relief

- Fostering social connections through ensemble playing and performances

3. Getting Started: Choosing the Right Violin

- Selecting an appropriate violin size for the child's age and physical stature

- Considering the quality and playability of the instrument

- Seeking guidance from a knowledgeable teacher or music specialist

4. The Basics of Violin Technique

- Holding the violin with proper posture and balance

- Understanding the parts of the violin and their functions

- Correctly positioning the left hand and fingers on the fingerboard

3

- Mastering the bow hold and producing a consistent sound

5. Structuring Violin Exercises for Children

- Starting with simple exercises to develop finger strength and flexibility

- Incorporating bowing exercises to improve control and tone production

- Gradually introducing scales and arpeggios to enhance technical skills

- Integrating music theory and sight-reading exercises for a well-rounded education

6. Tailoring Exercises to Suit Children's Learning Styles

- Making the learning process enjoyable through games and challenges

- Utilizing visual aids, diagrams, and interactive tools

- Incorporating ear training and improvisation activities

- Providing opportunities for ensemble playing and collaboration

7. Nurturing a Positive Learning Environment

- Encouraging regular practice routines and setting achievable goals

- Offering constructive feedback and praise for progress

5

- Creating a supportive and nurturing atmosphere during lessons and rehearsals

- Celebrating achievements and milestones along the learning journey

8. Parental Involvement and Support

- Communicating with the child's music teacher and staying informed about progress

- Creating a practice schedule and providing a quiet and dedicated practice space

- Attending performances and recitals to show support and appreciation

- Encouraging a love for music beyond violin exercises, such as listening to recordings and attending concerts

In conclusion, introducing children to violin exercises opens a world of musical possibilities. Through a structured and engaging approach, children can develop valuable skills, cultivate their musicality, and experience the joy of playing the violin. With parental support and guidance, the journey of learning the violin can be a fulfilling and transformative experience for children.

BENEFITS OF TEACHING VIOLIN TO CHILDREN

Teaching children to play the violin offers numerous benefits that extend beyond mere musical proficiency. The violin, with its rich and expressive sound, provides a platform for children to develop a wide range of skills and qualities that can positively impact their overall growth and development. Here are some extensive benefits of teaching violin to children:

1. Cognitive Development:

   - Enhances memory and concentration: Learning to play the violin requires children to memorize music, which strengthens their memory and concentration abilities.

8

- Improves problem-solving skills: Figuring out finger placements, bowing techniques, and reading sheet music promotes critical thinking and problem-solving skills.

- Develops multitasking skills: Playing the violin demands simultaneous coordination of various tasks, such as reading music, maintaining proper posture, and executing precise finger movements.

2. Physical Development:

- Enhances fine motor skills: Playing the violin involves intricate finger movements and bow control, promoting the development of fine motor skills and hand-eye coordination.

- Improves posture and body awareness: Proper violin technique encourages correct posture, alignment, and body awareness, leading to improved overall physical posture and control.

- Strengthens dexterity and finger independence: The complex finger movements required on the fingerboard strengthen dexterity and promote finger independence.

3. Emotional and Social Development:

- Fosters self-expression and creativity: Playing the violin allows children to express their emotions and creativity through music, providing an outlet for self-expression.

- Cultivates discipline and patience: Regular practice and dedication to

10

mastering the violin teach children discipline, patience, and perseverance, valuable life skills that can be applied in various areas.

- Builds self-confidence and self-esteem: Progressing in violin playing and performing in front of others boosts self-confidence and self-esteem, fostering a positive self-image.

- Nurtures empathy and teamwork: Participation in ensemble playing, such as orchestras or chamber groups, encourages collaboration, empathy, and teamwork skills.

4. Academic and Intellectual Benefits:

- Improves listening skills: Playing the violin requires attentive listening to pitch, tone, and rhythm, which

11

enhances auditory perception and listening skills.

   - Enhances mathematical abilities: The study of music theory, rhythms, and subdivisions supports the development of mathematical skills, including counting, timing, and pattern recognition.

   - Enhances linguistic abilities: Research suggests that musical training can have a positive impact on language development, including phonetic awareness, vocabulary acquisition, and reading comprehension.

5. Emotional Well-being and Stress Relief:

   - Provides emotional outlet: Playing the violin can serve as a means of emotional expression and stress relief, allowing children to channel their feelings into music.

- Promotes relaxation and mindfulness: Engaging in the act of playing the violin can induce a state of relaxation and mindfulness, reducing stress and promoting well-being.

6. Appreciation for Music and Cultural Enrichment:

- Exposes children to a diverse range of music: Learning the violin introduces children to various musical genres, styles, and composers, broadening their musical horizons.

- Fosters cultural appreciation: Studying the violin exposes children to different cultural traditions and musical heritage, fostering an appreciation for diversity and cultural understanding.

13

In conclusion, teaching the violin to children provides a multitude of benefits that extend far beyond the realm of music. From cognitive and physical development to emotional well-being and cultural enrichment, the violin offers a holistic learning experience that nurtures various aspects of a child's growth and development.

SETTING UP FOR SUCCESS: PREPARING THE VIOLIN AND BOW

Properly preparing the violin and bow is crucial for a child's success in learning to play the instrument. By ensuring that the violin and bow are in optimal condition, children can experience improved playability, sound quality, and overall comfort. Here are extensive guidelines for setting up the violin and bow for success:

1. Choosing a Suitable Violin:

- Selecting the appropriate size: Children should be equipped with a violin that matches their age, physical stature, and hand size. An ill-fitting violin can hinder their ability to play comfortably and progress effectively.

- Assessing the quality: It is essential to choose a violin of good quality that is well-constructed and produces a desirable sound. A high-quality instrument will inspire confidence and facilitate better learning outcomes.

2. Tuning the Violin:

- Understanding pitch and tuning: Introduce children to the concept of pitch and the importance of tuning the violin. Teach them how to use a tuner or rely on their ears to adjust the pegs or fine tuners until the strings are in tune.

- Encouraging regular tuning: Emphasize the significance of tuning the violin before every practice session or performance to develop their ear and maintain accurate intonation.

3. Checking the Violin Setup:

- Assessing the bridge: Ensure that the bridge is positioned correctly and standing upright between the f-holes. It should be neither too flat nor too angled, allowing for optimal string clearance and proper vibration transmission.

- Evaluating the soundpost: The soundpost, located inside the violin, should be standing upright and positioned correctly, supporting the tension of the strings and transmitting vibrations effectively.

- Inspecting the strings: Examine the condition of the strings regularly for signs of wear, fraying, or corrosion. Replace worn-out strings promptly to ensure consistent sound quality.

17

4. Preparing the Bow:

- Properly tightening the bow hair: Instruct children on how to loosen the bow screw before tightening the hair. Advise them to tighten the hair until it feels taut and remains parallel to the bow stick, allowing for optimal control and sound production.

- Applying rosin: Demonstrate how to apply rosin evenly along the bow hair. Explain its purpose in creating friction between the bow and strings, which produces sound. Encourage children to rosin the bow regularly to maintain optimal grip and sound quality.

5. Bow Care and Maintenance:

- Cleaning the bow: Teach children to wipe the bow stick with a clean cloth after each use to remove rosin buildup and oils from their hands. This maintains the integrity of the bow's materials and prevents damage.

- Protecting the bow hair: Instruct children to loosen the bow hair when not in use, preventing excessive tension that can lead to hair breakage. Encourage them to store the bow in a protective case or bow holder to safeguard it from accidental damage.

6. Creating a Suitable Playing Environment:

- Establishing a dedicated practice space: Help children create a

19

designated area for violin practice, free from distractions and with adequate lighting. Ensure that the space is well-ventilated and provides a comfortable temperature for optimal playing conditions.

- Maintaining proper humidity levels: The violin is sensitive to changes in humidity, which can affect its sound and structural integrity. Encourage children to use a humidifier or dehumidifier to maintain a stable humidity level that is suitable for their specific climate.

By paying attention to the setup of the violin and bow, children can begin their violin journey on the right foot. A well-prepared instrument promotes comfort, playability, and sound quality, enhancing their overall learning experience and setting the stage for success in their musical endeavors.

UNDERSTANDING BASIC VIOLIN TECHNIQUE

Mastering basic violin technique is essential for any aspiring violinist, including children. Building a solid foundation in technique lays the groundwork for musical development and enables students to progress effectively. Here is an extensive guide to understanding basic violin technique:

1. Proper Posture and Positioning:

 - Holding the violin: Teach children to hold the violin with their chin resting on the chinrest, ensuring a stable and secure grip. The left hand should support the neck of the violin, allowing freedom for finger movements.

- Maintaining an upright posture: Emphasize the importance of sitting or standing with a straight back, relaxed shoulders, and balanced weight distribution. Good posture promotes better control, tone production, and prevents physical strain.

2. Left Hand Technique:

- Finger placement and intonation: Instruct children to place their fingers directly behind the desired notes, applying the right amount of pressure to produce a clear and resonant sound. Encourage accurate intonation through listening and ear training.

- Finger independence and flexibility: Guide children in developing finger independence, allowing them to press down one finger while keeping the others relaxed and ready to move.

23

Promote exercises for finger strength, dexterity, and agility.

   - Shifting and vibrato: Introduce shifting techniques, teaching children to slide their fingers smoothly along the fingerboard to reach different positions. As they progress, gradually introduce the concept and practice of vibrato, a nuanced and expressive technique.

3. Right Hand Technique:

   - Bow hold: Demonstrate and assist children in achieving a proper bow hold, with the fingers curved and relaxed, and the thumb resting on the bow's grip. The bow should be held at a balanced angle, with the pinky providing stability.

- Bowing techniques: Teach children the fundamental bowing techniques such as whole bow strokes, half bow strokes, and short bow strokes. Emphasize the importance of maintaining a consistent bow speed, pressure, and contact point for even tone production.

- Bow direction and string crossings: Guide children to develop smooth bow changes and string crossings, ensuring seamless transitions between strings without interruptions or breaks in sound. Encourage them to visualize and anticipate the path of the bow.

- Dynamics and articulation: Introduce children to dynamics (soft and loud playing) and articulation (e.g., staccato, legato). Teach them how to control the bow speed, pressure, and contact point to achieve the desired expressive effects.

4. Bowing Exercises and Etudes:

   - Scale exercises: Introduce children to scales, starting with basic scales such as the G major and D major scales. Gradually progress to more advanced scales in different keys to develop finger and bowing coordination.

   - Bowing exercises: Incorporate bowing exercises that focus on specific techniques, such as bow distribution, spiccato, or string crossings. These exercises help children refine their control and precision.

   - Etudes: Introduce age-appropriate etudes that provide musical challenges and opportunities for technical development. Etudes help children develop musicality, phrasing, and advanced technical skills.

5. Posture and Technique Maintenance:

   - Regular self-evaluation: Teach children to monitor their posture and technique during practice sessions. Encourage them to identify and correct any tension, imbalances, or errors in their playing.

   - Slow and deliberate practice: Emphasize the importance of practicing slowly and deliberately, focusing on accuracy, tone quality, and technique. Gradually increase the tempo as skills improve.

   - Seek guidance from a teacher: Encourage children to work with a qualified violin teacher who can provide personalized guidance, correct technique, and offer constructive feedback to address specific challenges.

Understanding and developing basic violin technique is a gradual process that requires consistent practice, patience, and guidance. By focusing on proper posture, finger placement, bowing technique, and regular self-evaluation, children can establish a strong technical foundation that will serve as a springboard for their musical growth and artistic expression on the violin.

HOLDING THE VIOLIN

Learning how to hold the violin correctly is vital for any aspiring violinist, as it establishes a solid foundation for technique and allows for comfortable and efficient playing. Here is an extensive guide on holding the violin with proper technique and positioning:

1. Shoulder Rest or Chinrest:

   - Determine the need for a shoulder rest: Assess the individual child's anatomy and comfort level to determine whether a shoulder rest is necessary. A shoulder rest can provide support and improve stability, especially for children with shorter necks or those who require additional comfort.

29

- Choosing the right shoulder rest: If using a shoulder rest, select one that fits securely on the violin and provides the desired height and angle. It should allow the violin to rest comfortably on the collarbone and shoulder while maintaining stability.

2. *Chinrest Positioning:*

- Resting the chin: Instruct the child to position their chin on the chinrest, using the jawbone as a point of contact. The chinrest should provide stability without causing discomfort or restricting movement.

- Experimenting with chinrest models: Depending on the child's anatomy and comfort, different chinrest models may be more suitable. Encourage experimenting with various styles to find the one that offers the best balance of comfort and stability.

3. Left Hand and Arm Position:

- Supporting the neck of the violin: Teach the child to support the neck of the violin using the left hand. The thumb should be positioned opposite the middle and ring fingers, allowing for stability and control while keeping the fingers relaxed.

- Curving the fingers: Emphasize the importance of maintaining a curved shape with the left-hand fingers, ensuring that they are rounded and ready to press down on the strings when needed.

- Aligning the forearm: Guide the child to align the forearm parallel to the strings, allowing for optimal finger placement and minimizing tension in the left arm and hand.

- Avoiding excessive pressure: Encourage the child to apply only the necessary pressure on the strings to produce a clear sound, avoiding excessive finger pressure, which can cause unnecessary tension and fatigue.

4. Right Hand and Arm Position:

- Holding the bow: Instruct the child to hold the bow with a relaxed and flexible right hand. The thumb should rest on the grip, slightly bent, while the fingers curve naturally around the bow stick.

- Balancing the bow: Guide the child to find the balance point of the bow, which is typically located slightly closer to the frog (lower part of the bow) than the tip. This balance allows for optimal control and maneuverability.

   - Aligning the bow: Encourage the child to align the bow parallel to the bridge, ensuring a consistent and even contact point on the strings for a balanced and resonant sound.

   - Maintaining a relaxed arm: Emphasize the importance of a relaxed right arm and hand, avoiding excessive tension or gripping of the bow that can hinder fluid bowing and sound production.

5. Regular Self-Evaluation and Adjustment:

   - Encouraging self-awareness: Teach the child to be aware of their own body and sensations while playing, regularly checking for any discomfort, tension, or imbalances in their posture or hand positions.

   - Making adjustments: Instruct the child to make necessary adjustments to their chinrest, shoulder rest (if used), and hand positions to ensure comfort, stability, and freedom of movement. Small changes can make a significant difference in playing comfort and technique.

Remember, it is essential for children to work closely with a qualified violin teacher who can provide personalized guidance, make necessary adjustments, and correct any potential issues in their holding and playing techniques. By mastering proper violin holding technique, children can develop a solid foundation for their violin journey, facilitating improved

comfort, control, and musical
expression.

HOLDING THE BOW

Mastering the proper technique for holding the bow is crucial for violinists, as it directly influences tone production, control, and overall musical expression. Here is an extensive guide on holding the bow with proper technique and positioning:

1. Hand Position:

   - Placement of the bow in the hand: Instruct the child to position the bow in the right hand, resting the thumb on the grip and curving the fingers naturally around the bow stick. The pinky should be resting on the frog, providing stability.

   - Relaxed and flexible hand: Emphasize the importance of

36

maintaining a relaxed and flexible hand while holding the bow. Tension in the hand can hinder free movement and affect tone quality.

2. Bow Grip:

- The "V" shape grip: Teach the child to create a "V" shape between the thumb and index finger, with the thumb slightly bent and the index finger resting on the bow stick opposite the thumb.

- Curving the other fingers: Instruct the child to curve the remaining fingers around the bow stick, allowing for a secure and comfortable grip. The middle, ring, and pinky fingers should rest gently on the bow stick without gripping too tightly.

- Avoiding excessive pressure: Emphasize using only the necessary pressure to maintain control and produce a clear sound. Excessive pressure can result in a harsh tone and unnecessary tension in the hand.

3. Bow Angle and Contact Point:

   - Proper bow angle: Guide the child to maintain a consistent bow angle relative to the strings. The bow should be positioned parallel to the bridge, allowing for optimal contact with the strings.

   - Finding the contact point: Instruct the child to explore different areas between the bridge and fingerboard to find the sweet spot where the bow produces the desired tone quality. Encourage experimentation and listening to the resulting sound.

4. Bow Arm and Wrist:

- Relaxed bow arm: Emphasize the importance of a relaxed and fluid bow arm. The arm should be free of tension, allowing for smooth and controlled bowing movements.

- Alignment of the bow arm: Guide the child to align the bow arm with the strings, maintaining a straight line from the elbow to the bow.

- Flexible wrist: Instruct the child to maintain a flexible wrist, allowing for subtle adjustments in bow angle and pressure. The wrist should neither be rigid nor excessively bent.

5. Bowing Motion:

  - Whole bow strokes: Teach the child to practice whole bow strokes, which involve smoothly moving the bow from the frog to the tip or vice versa. Emphasize maintaining a consistent bow speed and pressure throughout the stroke.

  - Half and short bow strokes: Introduce half bow and short bow strokes to develop control and precision. These bowing techniques require adjusting the speed and pressure accordingly to create even and controlled sound.

6. Regular Self-Evaluation and Adjustment:

  - Encouraging self-awareness: Teach the child to be aware of their bowing technique and the sensations in their hand and arm while playing. Regularly check for any tension, imbalances, or discomfort and make necessary adjustments.

- Seeking guidance from a teacher: It is crucial for the child to work closely with a qualified violin teacher who can provide personalized guidance, correct any potential issues in their bow hold, and offer constructive feedback to improve their technique.

By mastering the proper bow hold and technique, children can develop a foundation for expressive and controlled violin playing. Remember to encourage regular practice, self-evaluation, and guidance from a qualified teacher to refine and develop their bowing skills further.

PLACING FINGERS ON THE STRINGS

When learning the violin, understanding how to place the fingers correctly on the strings is crucial for accurate intonation and producing clear and resonant notes. Here is an extensive guide on placing fingers on the strings with proper technique and positioning:

1. Hand and Finger Placement:

   - Hand position: Instruct the child to maintain a relaxed and natural hand position. The hand should be slightly curved, with the fingers gently rounded and ready to press down on the strings when needed.

42

- Alignment with the fingerboard: Guide the child to align their fingers parallel to the fingerboard, ensuring that they are positioned directly behind the desired notes.

- Avoiding excessive tension: Emphasize the importance of applying only the necessary pressure on the strings to produce a clear sound. Excessive finger pressure can cause unnecessary tension and fatigue.

2. Finger Independence and Flexibility:

- Developing finger independence: Teach the child to move each finger independently of the others, allowing for precise and controlled finger placement. Encourage exercises that isolate individual fingers to enhance independence and coordination.

43

- Finger flexibility: Emphasize keeping the fingers relaxed and flexible while placing them on the strings. Stiff or tense fingers can hinder accurate intonation and impede smooth transitions between notes.

3. Intonation and Listening Skills:

- Ear training: Promote ear training by encouraging the child to listen carefully to the pitch and quality of the notes they produce. Help them develop a keen sense of relative pitch and the ability to recognize when a note is in tune or not.

- Visualizing finger placement: Guide the child to visualize the positions of the notes on the fingerboard, using reference points such as tape or markers initially, if needed. Over time, they should aim to rely less on visual aids and more on their ears and muscle memory.

4. Shifting and Position Changes:

- Shifting technique: Introduce shifting techniques to the child as they progress. Teach them how to slide their fingers smoothly along the fingerboard to reach different positions. Emphasize accuracy, maintaining a consistent tone, and smooth transitions during shifts.

- Maintaining finger position in different positions: Instruct the child to maintain proper finger placement and alignment in various positions on the fingerboard. Encourage them to be mindful of their hand and finger position when moving to higher or lower positions.

5. Regular Self-Evaluation and Adjustment:

- Self-assessment: Teach the child to evaluate their finger placement and intonation while practicing. Encourage them to listen critically to their playing and make necessary adjustments to achieve accurate intonation.

- Seeking guidance from a teacher: It is essential for the child to work closely with a qualified violin teacher who can provide personalized guidance, correct any potential issues in their finger placement, and offer constructive feedback to improve their intonation.

By mastering proper finger placement and intonation, children can develop a foundation for accurate and expressive violin playing. Encourage regular practice, self-evaluation, and guidance from a qualified teacher to refine and strengthen their finger technique on the instrument.

DEVELOPING PROPER POSTURE AND BODY POSITION

Establishing and maintaining proper posture and body position is fundamental for violinists, as it facilitates comfort, freedom of movement, and optimal technique. Here is an extensive guide on developing proper posture and body position for violin playing:

1. Standing Position:

   - Balanced stance: Instruct the child to stand with their feet shoulder-width apart, ensuring a balanced and stable foundation. The weight distribution should be evenly distributed between both feet.

48

- Alignment: Guide the child to align their body vertically, with the head, neck, spine, and hips in a straight line. Encourage them to maintain a relaxed and upright posture throughout their playing.

2. Shoulder and Upper Body Position:

- Relaxed shoulders: Emphasize the importance of keeping the shoulders relaxed and downward. Tension in the shoulders can hinder freedom of movement and cause discomfort.

- Balanced upper body: Instruct the child to maintain a balanced upper body position, centered over the feet. Avoid excessive leaning or tilting to either side.

- Natural curvature of the spine: Encourage the child to maintain the natural curvature of the spine, with a

49

slight inward curve in the lower back. Avoid slouching or overarching the back.

3. Head and Neck Position:

  - Alignment of the head and neck: Guide the child to align their head and neck with their spine, keeping it in a neutral position. The chin should be level, and the head should not be tilted or excessively raised.

  - Resting the chin: Instruct the child to rest their chin comfortably on the chinrest, using the jawbone as a point of contact. The head should be stable but not rigid, allowing for freedom of movement.

4. Violin and Bow Hold:

   - Holding the violin: Teach the child to hold the violin with their left hand and support it using the collarbone and shoulder. Emphasize a relaxed left hand and arm position to allow for flexibility and ease of movement.

   - Holding the bow: Guide the child to hold the bow with a relaxed and flexible right hand. The thumb should rest on the grip, slightly bent, while the fingers curve naturally around the bow stick. Encourage a relaxed and fluid right arm and wrist.

5. Regular Self-Evaluation and Adjustment:

   - Body awareness: Teach the child to develop body awareness while playing, regularly checking for any tension, discomfort, or imbalances in their posture or body position.

- Making adjustments: Instruct the child to make necessary adjustments to their posture and body position to ensure comfort, stability, and freedom of movement. Small changes can make a significant difference in playing comfort and technique.

6. Seeking Guidance from a Teacher:

- Working with a teacher: It is crucial for the child to work closely with a qualified violin teacher who can provide personalized guidance, correct any potential issues in their posture and body position, and offer constructive feedback to improve their technique.

- Teacher-assisted adjustments: A teacher can assist in making adjustments to the child's posture and body position, ensuring optimal alignment and comfort. They can also provide guidance on exercises and stretches to promote healthy playing habits and prevent injuries.

By developing proper posture and body position, children can establish a solid foundation for their violin playing. Encourage regular practice, self-evaluation, and guidance from a qualified teacher to refine and maintain proper posture and body position throughout their violin journey.

SITTING OR STANDING POSITION

When it comes to violin playing, finding the right sitting or standing position is crucial for achieving comfort, stability, and optimal technique. Here is an extensive guide on establishing the proper sitting or standing position for playing the violin:

1. Sitting Position:

   - Chair selection: Choose a chair that allows the child to sit with their feet flat on the ground comfortably. The chair should provide adequate support and stability.

   - Balanced posture: Instruct the child to sit with an upright and balanced posture. Their weight should be evenly distributed on both hips, and the spine should be aligned in a straight but relaxed manner.

- Feet position: Encourage the child to place both feet flat on the ground, shoulder-width apart. This provides a stable foundation and helps maintain balance during playing.

2. Standing Position:

- Balanced stance: Instruct the child to stand with their feet shoulder-width apart, ensuring a balanced and stable foundation. The weight distribution should be evenly distributed between both feet.

- Alignment: Guide the child to align their body vertically, with the head, neck, spine, and hips in a straight line. Encourage them to maintain a relaxed and upright posture throughout their playing.

3. Upper Body Position:

- Relaxed shoulders: Emphasize the importance of keeping the shoulders relaxed and downward. Tension in the shoulders can hinder freedom of movement and cause discomfort.

- Balanced upper body: Instruct the child to maintain a balanced upper body position, centered over the feet. Avoid excessive leaning or tilting to either side.

- Natural curvature of the spine: Encourage the child to maintain the natural curvature of the spine, with a slight inward curve in the lower back. Avoid slouching or overarching the back.

4. Head and Neck Position:

- Alignment of the head and neck: Guide the child to align their head and neck with their spine, keeping it in a neutral position. The chin should be level, and the head should not be tilted or excessively raised.

- Resting the chin: Instruct the child to rest their chin comfortably on the chinrest or shoulder rest, using the jawbone as a point of contact. The head should be stable but not rigid, allowing for freedom of movement.

5. Regular Self-Evaluation and Adjustment:

- Body awareness: Teach the child to develop body awareness while playing,

57

regularly checking for any tension, discomfort, or imbalances in their posture or body position.

   - Making adjustments: Instruct the child to make necessary adjustments to their posture and body position to ensure comfort, stability, and freedom of movement. Small changes can make a significant difference in playing comfort and technique.

6. Seeking Guidance from a Teacher:

   - Working with a teacher: It is crucial for the child to work closely with a qualified violin teacher who can provide personalized guidance, correct any potential issues in their posture and body position, and offer constructive feedback to improve their technique.

- Teacher-assisted adjustments: A teacher can assist in making adjustments to the child's posture and body position, ensuring optimal alignment and comfort. They can also provide guidance on exercises and stretches to promote healthy playing habits and prevent injuries.

By finding the proper sitting or standing position, children can establish a solid foundation for their violin playing. Encourage regular practice, self-evaluation, and guidance from a qualified teacher to refine and maintain proper posture and body position throughout their violin journey.

ALIGNING THE BODY AND INSTRUMENT

Proper alignment between the body and the instrument is crucial for violinists to achieve balance, connection, and optimal technique. Here is an extensive guide on aligning the body and instrument for violin playing:

1. Establishing a Solid Foundation:

- Body positioning: Instruct the child to stand or sit with an upright and balanced posture. The head, neck, spine, and hips should be aligned in a straight line.

- Feet or chair position: Ensure that the child's feet are flat on the ground if sitting or shoulder-width apart if

60

standing. If using a chair, it should provide stability and support.

- Distributing weight: Encourage the child to distribute their weight evenly between both feet or both hips, fostering a stable foundation.

2. Aligning the Violin:

- Chinrest and shoulder rest: Ensure that the child's chinrest and shoulder rest (if used) are properly adjusted for their individual physique. The chinrest should allow the child to comfortably rest their chin on it while maintaining a neutral head position.

- Violin position: Guide the child to position the violin in front of their body, parallel to the floor. The scroll should be elevated slightly above the shoulder level to facilitate a comfortable left hand position.

   - Use of a mirror: Utilize a mirror during practice sessions to help the child visually assess the alignment of their instrument with their body. This visual feedback can aid in making necessary adjustments.

3. Hand and Arm Alignment:

   - Left hand position: Instruct the child to position their left hand comfortably around the neck of the violin, with the fingers rounded and ready to press down on the strings. The hand should be aligned with the fingerboard to facilitate accurate finger placement.

   - Right arm position: Guide the child to maintain a relaxed and natural right arm position. The forearm should be parallel to the strings, allowing for smooth bowing motion. Encourage a flexible and supple wrist for optimal bow control.

4. Connection with the Body:

- Body awareness: Teach the child to develop body awareness while playing, paying attention to any tension, discomfort, or imbalances. Encourage them to maintain a sense of connection between their body and the instrument.

- Relaxation and freedom of movement: Emphasize the importance of staying relaxed throughout the body, particularly in the shoulders, arms, and hands. Tension can hinder proper alignment and impede fluid technique.

- Regular self-evaluation: Instruct the child to regularly evaluate their body and instrument alignment during practice sessions. Encourage them to make any necessary adjustments to ensure comfort, balance, and a seamless connection.

5. Seeking Guidance from a Teacher:

- Working with a teacher: It is essential for the child to work closely with a qualified violin teacher who can provide personalized guidance, correct any potential issues in their body and instrument alignment, and offer constructive feedback to improve their technique.

- Teacher-assisted adjustments: A teacher can assist in aligning the child's body and instrument, ensuring optimal balance and connection. They can also provide guidance on exercises and drills to strengthen the alignment and enhance overall playing performance.

By aligning the body and instrument, children can establish a foundation for balanced and connected violin playing. Encourage regular practice, self-evaluation, and guidance from a qualified teacher to refine and maintain proper alignment throughout their violin journey.

WARM-UP EXERCISES FOR FINGERS AND HANDS

Performing warm-up exercises for the fingers and hands is essential for violinists to prepare their muscles, increase blood flow, and enhance dexterity and flexibility. Here is an extensive guide on warm-up exercises for fingers and hands in violin playing:

1. Finger Stretches:

- Finger spreads: Begin by extending the fingers of both hands wide apart, then slowly bring them together, touching each fingertip to the corresponding fingertip of the opposite hand. Repeat this exercise several times, focusing on maintaining control and precision.

- Finger rolls: Roll the fingers of both hands in a circular motion, starting from the base knuckle and moving towards the fingertips. Perform this exercise in both clockwise and counterclockwise directions, promoting flexibility and joint mobility.

2. Finger Independence Exercises:

- Finger lifts: Place the fingers of the left hand on a flat surface, such as a table, and lift each finger individually, starting from the pinky finger to the index finger. Repeat this exercise multiple times, ensuring each finger is lifted smoothly and independently.

- Finger taps: Tap the fingers of the left hand on a table or any other surface, one finger at a time, in a sequential order, such as pinky, ring, middle, index. Gradually increase the

67

speed while maintaining accuracy and control.

3. Finger Strength and Control:

- Finger presses: Place the fingers of the left hand on a flat surface, and press each finger down individually, starting from the index finger to the pinky finger. Focus on applying consistent pressure and releasing the finger with control.

- Finger spider crawl: Starting with the pinky finger, lift each finger individually, keeping the previous finger down. Repeat this exercise, gradually moving towards the index finger. This exercise strengthens the fingers and promotes control and coordination.

4. Hand and Wrist Stretches:

- Wrist circles: Rotate the wrists in a circular motion, both clockwise and counterclockwise. This exercise helps loosen the wrists and improves flexibility.

- Hand stretches: Extend the arm forward, palm facing down, and gently pull the fingers back with the other hand, stretching the palm and fingers. Hold the stretch for a few seconds and repeat with the other hand. This stretch targets the flexor muscles in the hand and promotes flexibility.

5. Scales and Arpeggios:

- Play scales and arpeggios: Practice scales and arpeggios in different keys and positions to warm up the fingers and promote finger independence,

69

coordination, and agility. Start slowly and gradually increase the tempo as the fingers warm up.

6. *Gradual Tempo Increase:*

   - Begin with slow tempo: When starting the warm-up exercises, begin with a slow tempo to allow the fingers and hands to gradually warm up and adapt to the movements.

   - Increase tempo gradually: As the fingers and hands become more responsive and flexible, gradually increase the speed and intensity of the exercises. However, always prioritize accuracy and control over speed.

7. Listening to the Body:

- Pay attention to fatigue or discomfort: While performing warm-up exercises, listen to your body and be mindful of any signs of fatigue, tension, or discomfort. If necessary, take short breaks or modify the exercises to suit your individual needs.

Remember, warm-up exercises are not only beneficial for preparing the fingers and hands but also for focusing the mind and establishing a positive mindset. Incorporate these warm-up exercises into your regular practice routine to promote dexterity, flexibility, and overall finger and hand health in violin playing.

FINGER STRETCHING AND FLEXING

Finger stretching and flexing exercises play a crucial role in promoting mobility, flexibility, and agility in violin playing. Here is an extensive guide on finger stretching and flexing exercises:

1. Individual Finger Stretches:

- Finger Extension: Start with the left hand palm facing up. Gently push the fingers of the left hand back towards the wrist using the fingers of the right hand. Hold each finger individually for a few seconds, focusing on stretching and extending the joints. Repeat with the right hand.

- Finger Flexion: Begin with the left hand palm facing down. Use the right hand to gently pull each finger of the left hand towards the palm, creating a flexion at the joints. Hold each finger individually for a few seconds, emphasizing the stretch. Repeat with the right hand.

2. Finger-to-Palm Stretches:

- Finger-to-Palm Touch: Place the left hand palm facing up. Use the right hand to press each finger down towards the palm, aiming to touch the base of the fingers to the palm. Hold each finger individually for a few seconds, feeling the stretch in the fingers and palm. Repeat with the right hand.

3. Finger Independence Exercises:

   - Finger Lifts: Begin with the left hand palm facing up. Lift each finger individually, starting from the pinky finger to the index finger, while keeping the other fingers down on a flat surface. Focus on maintaining control and precision in each finger movement. Repeat with the right hand.

   - Finger Taps: Start with the left hand palm facing down. One at a time, tap each finger of the left hand on a flat surface, focusing on quick and independent movements. Gradually increase the speed while maintaining accuracy. Repeat with the right hand.

4. Finger Strength and Control:

   - Finger Presses: Place the left hand fingers on a flat surface, such as a table. Press each finger down individually, starting from the index finger to the pinky finger. Focus on applying consistent pressure and releasing the finger with control. Repeat with the right hand.

   - Finger Spider Crawl: Starting with the pinky finger, lift each finger individually while keeping the previous finger down. Repeat this exercise, gradually moving towards the index finger. This exercise strengthens the fingers and promotes control and coordination. Repeat with the right hand.

5. Finger Rolling and Circles:

   - Finger Rolls: Roll the fingers of both hands in a circular motion, starting from the base knuckle and moving towards the fingertips. Perform this exercise in both clockwise and counterclockwise directions, promoting flexibility and joint mobility.

   - Finger Circles: Make small circles with each finger individually, starting from the base knuckle and moving towards the fingertips. Perform this exercise in both clockwise and counterclockwise directions, focusing on smooth and controlled movements. Repeat with the other hand.

6. *Finger Stretching Tools:*

   - Finger Bands: Utilize finger resistance bands or rubber bands to provide gentle resistance while stretching the fingers. Place the band around the fingertips and open the fingers against the resistance, promoting finger extension and flexibility.

76

- Finger Massages: Incorporate finger massages using a tennis ball or a foam roller. Roll the ball or roller gently along the palm and fingers, applying pressure to release tension and increase blood circulation.

7. Regular Practice and Gradual Progression:

- Frequency: Include finger stretching and flexing exercises in your regular practice routine, ideally at the beginning to warm up the fingers and prepare them for playing.

- Gradual Progression: Start with gentle stretches and movements, gradually increasing the intensity and range of motion over time. Avoid excessive force or discomfort, and listen to your body's limits.

By incorporating finger stretching and flexing exercises into your practice routine, you can enhance the mobility, flexibility, and agility of your fingers, supporting improved technique and ease of playing in the context of violin performance.

HAND COORDINATION DRILLS

Developing hand coordination is essential for violinists to achieve precise and fluid movements while playing. Here is an extensive guide on hand coordination drills:

1. Finger Independence Exercises:

   - Finger Lifts: Place the left hand fingers on a flat surface, such as a table. Lift each finger individually, starting from the pinky finger to the index finger, while keeping the other fingers down. Focus on maintaining control and precision. Repeat with the right hand.

   - Finger Taps: Start with the left hand palm facing down. One at a time, tap each finger of the left hand on a flat surface, focusing on quick and independent movements. Gradually increase the speed while maintaining accuracy. Repeat with the right hand.

2. String Crossing Exercises:

- String Skipping: Using the bow, practice crossing from one string to another in a controlled manner. Start with adjacent strings and gradually progress to skipping strings. Focus on maintaining a consistent bow angle and smooth transitions.

- String Changing: Play a series of notes on one string and then switch to another string. Gradually increase the speed and complexity of the string changes, ensuring accuracy and minimizing unwanted noise.

3. Bowing and Finger Synchronization:

- Bow Retakes: Practice playing a note and then lifting the bow off the string, followed by placing it back on the string to play the next note. Focus on synchronized movements between the bowing hand and the finger placement of the left hand.

- Bow Lifts: Lift the bow off the string after each note, emphasizing a clear separation between notes. This exercise promotes clean articulation and coordination between the bowing and fingering actions.

4. Shifting Exercises:

- Position Shifting: Practice shifting from one position to another on the fingerboard, maintaining accuracy and intonation. Start with small shifts and gradually increase the distance. Focus on smooth and controlled movements of both the left hand and the bowing hand.

- Shifting with Open Strings: Incorporate open strings into shifting exercises. Play a note on one string, shift to a different position while maintaining an open string drone, and then play a note on the new position. This exercise improves hand coordination during position shifts.

5. Rhythm Exercises:

- Bowing and Fingering Patterns: Practice rhythmic bowing and fingering patterns, such as slurs, staccatos, and spiccato. Focus on precise coordination between the bowing hand and the finger movements on the left hand, maintaining a consistent pulse and rhythm.

- Bowing Variations: Experiment with different bowing techniques, such as bow accents, bow divisions, and bowing patterns across strings. These exercises improve hand coordination while exploring various bowing possibilities.

6. Double Stops and Chords:

  - Double Stop Exercises: Practice playing double stops (two notes played simultaneously) on different string combinations. Focus on maintaining evenness and coordination between the fingers of the left hand.

  - Chord Progressions: Play chord progressions on the violin, focusing on coordinating both hands to produce clean and balanced chord sounds. Gradually increase the complexity of the chord progressions to challenge hand coordination further.

7. Slow Practice and Gradual Progression:

  - Slow Practice: Start by practicing coordination drills at a slow tempo, focusing on accuracy and

84

synchronization between the hands. Pay attention to proper technique and clarity of sound.

- Gradual Progression: As coordination improves, gradually increase the speed and complexity of the drills. Challenge yourself with more intricate patterns, faster tempos, and advanced techniques. However, always prioritize accuracy and control over speed.

Consistent practice of hand coordination drills will enhance your dexterity, control, and precision in violin playing. Incorporate these exercises into your regular practice routine to develop smooth and synchronized movements between your hands, ultimately improving your overall performance on the violin.

BOWING EXERCISES FOR CONTROL AND ARTICULATION

Bowing exercises are crucial for young violinists to develop control, precision, and articulation in their playing. Here is an extensive guide on bowing exercises tailored for children:

1. Bow Hold Refinement:

  - Bow Hold Check: Begin by ensuring a proper bow hold. Guide the child's hand into the correct position, emphasizing a relaxed grip with curved fingers. Practice holding the bow and making small bow strokes to reinforce the correct hand position.

2. Whole Bow Control:

  - Full Bow Strokes: Encourage the child to perform long, smooth bow strokes using the entire length of the bow. Focus on maintaining a consistent tone and even pressure throughout the stroke. Gradually increase the speed and work on sustaining a steady sound.

3. Bow Distribution:

  - Bow Division Exercises: Introduce the concept of bow division by dividing the bow into equal sections (e.g., thirds or quarters). Practice playing scales or simple melodies, starting with one bow division and gradually increasing the number. This exercise develops control and awareness of bow distribution.

4. Articulation and Bowing Techniques:

  - Staccato Bowing: Teach the child to perform short, detached notes using quick, controlled bow movements. Practice staccato on open strings and then progress to playing simple melodies. Emphasize clear separation between notes while maintaining a consistent sound quality.

  - Legato Bowing: Guide the child in achieving smooth, connected bow strokes. Encourage them to produce a seamless sound by maintaining a steady bow speed and fluid finger movements on the left hand. Practice legato playing on scales and melodic passages.

  - Spiccato Bowing: Introduce spiccato, a bouncing bow technique.

89

Start with gentle, controlled bounces close to the string and gradually increase the height and speed. Focus on maintaining a relaxed bow hand and wrist to achieve a clear and controlled spiccato sound.

5. *String Crossings:*

- String Crossing Exercises: Practice crossing from one string to another smoothly and accurately. Start with open strings, and then progress to playing scales, arpeggios, or simple tunes that involve string crossings. Encourage the child to maintain a consistent bow angle and avoid unwanted noise.

- String Changing Drills: Focus on transitioning from one string to another efficiently. Practice shifting between strings while maintaining a steady sound and smooth bow movement. Gradually increase the speed and complexity of the string changes.

6. *Dynamic Control:*

- Crescendo-Decrescendo: Teach the child to control the volume of their playing. Begin with simple exercises, such as playing a note with a crescendo (gradually getting louder) and then a decrescendo (gradually getting softer). Encourage them to listen attentively and adjust their bow speed and pressure accordingly.

- Dynamic Contrasts: Practice playing melodies with contrasting dynamics, such as playing one phrase softly and the next phrase loudly. Help the child understand the importance of bow control and the impact it has on expression and musicality.

7. *Practice Strategies:*

- Slow Practice: Encourage the child to practice bowing exercises and techniques at a slow tempo initially. This allows them to focus on proper technique, control, and coordination between the bowing hand and the left hand.

- Repetition and Variation: Emphasize the importance of repetition to reinforce muscle memory and build consistency. Encourage the child to practice bowing exercises regularly while incorporating variations in dynamics, speed, and bowing techniques.

By incorporating these bowing exercises into their practice routine, young violinists can develop control, articulation, and technical proficiency. Encourage them to approach these exercises with patience, focus, and a playful attitude, fostering a strong foundation for their violin playing journey.

BOWING DIRECTION AND PRESSURE

Understanding bowing direction and pressure is essential for young violinists to achieve control and expressiveness in their playing. Here is an extensive guide on bowing direction and pressure tailored for children:

1. Bowing Direction:

   - Down-Bow and Up-Bow: Explain to the child the concept of down-bow (bowing from frog to tip) and up-bow (bowing from tip to frog). Emphasize the importance of maintaining a straight bow path parallel to the bridge.

   - Bowing Exercises: Practice playing open strings, scales, or simple melodies while focusing on consistent and accurate bowing direction. Encourage the child to visually track the bow's path and develop muscle memory for smooth bow changes.

2. *Bowing Pressure:*

- Bowing Pressure Awareness: Teach the child to be aware of the pressure applied to the strings. Explain that different dynamics and tonal qualities can be achieved by adjusting bowing pressure.

- Dynamic Control Exercises: Practice playing simple melodies with varying dynamics, such as playing softly (light bow pressure) and loudly (firm bow pressure). Encourage the child to listen attentively and adjust the pressure to achieve the desired dynamic effect.

95

3. Bowing Techniques for Expression:

 - Legato and Smooth Bowing: Guide the child in achieving a smooth, connected sound by maintaining a consistent bow speed and fluid finger movements on the left hand. Encourage them to explore dynamic nuances within legato passages.

 - Staccato and Detached Bowing: Teach the child to perform clear, separated notes using controlled bowing motions. Practice staccato on open strings and then progress to playing simple melodies with staccato markings. Help them understand how bow pressure affects the articulation and clarity of the notes.

 - Expressive Bowing: Introduce the concept of expressive bowing techniques, such as vibrato, bow vibrato, and bow accents. Demonstrate and guide the child in incorporating these techniques to add depth and emotion to their playing.

4. Bowing Exercises for Control:

- Bowing Control Drills: Practice bowing exercises that focus on control and precision. These can include bowing on a single string, playing scales, or performing string crossings with accurate bow changes. Emphasize the importance of maintaining a consistent bow pressure throughout the exercises.

- Bowing Variations: Explore different bowing patterns, such as bow division exercises, where the bow is divided into equal sections. Encourage the child to experiment with different

97

bowing pressures within these patterns to develop control and consistency.

5. *Guided Practice Strategies:*

- Visual and Verbal Cues: Use visual aids, such as colored stickers on the bow or fingerboard, to reinforce bowing direction and pressure concepts. Provide verbal reminders during practice sessions to help the child maintain awareness of their bowing technique.

- Teacher Feedback: Regularly provide constructive feedback to the child, addressing their bowing direction and pressure. Encourage them to ask questions and seek clarification to deepen their understanding and refine their technique.

6. *Musical Interpretation:*

- Phrasing and Dynamics: Help the child understand how bowing direction and pressure contribute to musical phrasing and dynamics. Practice playing melodies with varying dynamics, exploring expressive possibilities by adjusting bow pressure and direction accordingly.

- Musical Expression Exercises: Encourage the child to explore different musical styles and genres. Guide them in incorporating appropriate bowing techniques, dynamics, and expression to bring out the character and emotion of the music they are playing.

By focusing on bowing direction and pressure, young violinists can develop control, expression, and tonal variety in their playing. Through consistent practice and guidance, they will develop a nuanced understanding of how bowing techniques influence their musical performance, ultimately enhancing their overall violin playing skills.

BOWING SPEED AND DYNAMICS

Understanding bowing speed and dynamics is crucial for young violinists to express themselves and bring out the musicality in their playing. Here is an extensive guide on bowing speed and dynamics tailored for children:

1. Bowing Speed:

  - Slow Bowing: Teach the child the importance of slow bowing for developing control, accuracy, and tone production. Encourage them to practice playing long, sustained notes or simple melodies at a slow tempo, focusing on maintaining a consistent bow speed throughout.

101

- Fast Bowing: Introduce the concept of fast bowing, which involves quick and nimble bow movements. Guide the child in practicing short, rapid bow strokes on open strings or simple exercises. Emphasize the importance of maintaining control and clarity even at higher speeds.

2. Dynamics:

- Soft Dynamics: Teach the child how to produce a soft, delicate sound by reducing bow pressure and speed. Practice playing passages or melodies softly, focusing on achieving a gentle and controlled tone. Encourage them to experiment with different levels of softness to develop a range of dynamic expression.

- Loud Dynamics: Guide the child in producing a strong, powerful sound by increasing bow pressure and speed. Practice playing passages or melodies loudly, focusing on maintaining control and avoiding a harsh or scratchy tone. Help them explore different levels of loudness while maintaining a clear and resonant sound.

- Dynamic Contrasts: Teach the child how to transition smoothly between soft and loud dynamics within a piece of music. Practice playing phrases or sections with gradual dynamic changes, emphasizing the importance of adjusting both bow speed and pressure to achieve a seamless transition.

3. Bowing Exercises for Speed and Dynamics:

- Scale Variations: Practice scales in different bowing speeds, starting from slow and gradually increasing the tempo. Encourage the child to maintain control and precision while adjusting the bow speed accordingly.

- Dynamic Scale Exercises: Incorporate dynamic variations into scale practice. Explore playing scales with crescendos (gradually getting louder) and decrescendos (gradually getting softer) within a single bow stroke. This exercise helps develop control over both bow speed and dynamics.

- Melodic Studies: Choose melodic studies or etudes that specifically focus on bowing speed and dynamics. These exercises often contain passages that require rapid bowing or demand subtle dynamic changes. Work on these pieces together, guiding the child to achieve the desired musical expression.

4. Musical Interpretation:

- Expression Markings: Teach the child to interpret expression markings in the music score, such as crescendo, decrescendo, forte, piano, and other dynamic indications. Guide them in incorporating appropriate bowing speed and pressure adjustments to bring out the intended musical expression.

- Phrasing and Articulation: Help the child understand how bowing speed and dynamics contribute to phrasing and articulation. Practice playing melodies with different phrasing styles, emphasizing the connection between bowing speed, dynamics, and musical shaping.

5. Guided Practice Strategies:

- Listening Exercises: Encourage the child to listen to professional violinists' performances, focusing on their use of bowing speed and dynamics to bring out the musicality of the pieces. Discuss and analyze these performances together, helping the child develop a discerning ear for musical expression.

- Experimentation and Exploration: Encourage the child to experiment with different bowing speeds and dynamics during their practice sessions. Provide a supportive environment that allows them to explore and discover their own musical ideas while providing guidance and feedback.

By focusing on bowing speed and dynamics, young violinists can develop

106

a sense of musicality, expression, and control in their playing. Through consistent practice, listening, and guided exploration, they will develop the skills necessary to bring out the emotional depth and beauty of the music they perform.

LEFT HAND EXERCISES FOR FINGER DEXTERITY AND ACCURACY

Developing finger dexterity and accuracy in the left hand is crucial for young violinists to navigate the fingerboard with precision and fluency. Here is an extensive guide on left hand exercises tailored for children:

1. Finger Placement and Placement Accuracy:

- Finger Tapping: Teach the child to tap each finger individually on the fingerboard, focusing on placing the fingertips accurately on the intended notes. Start with simple exercises, such as tapping one finger per string, and gradually progress to more complex patterns.

- Finger Stretching: Help the child stretch their fingers by practicing exercises that involve placing fingers on adjacent strings simultaneously. Guide them in maintaining proper hand and finger positions while stretching comfortably to reach the desired notes.

2. Finger Independence and Mobility:

- Finger Lifts: Encourage the child to practice lifting and placing each finger independently on the fingerboard while keeping the other fingers down. This exercise promotes finger independence, strengthens finger muscles, and improves coordination.

- Finger Sequences: Guide the child in playing sequences of notes using different finger combinations. Start with simple patterns, such as 1-2-3-4 or 4-3-2-1, and gradually introduce more complex sequences. Emphasize accuracy, speed, and smooth transitions between fingers.

3. Finger Strength and Finger Pressure Control:

- Finger Pressure Exercises: Encourage the child to practice applying consistent finger pressure to the strings. Start with simple exercises, such as playing open strings with each finger, and progress to more intricate exercises involving scales, arpeggios, or melodies. Focus on producing a clear and resonant sound with controlled finger pressure.

- Finger Push-Ups: Demonstrate and guide the child in performing finger push-ups, where each finger is pressed down on the fingerboard one at a time and lifted up again. This exercise helps develop finger strength, control, and endurance.

4. Finger Agility and Speed:

- Finger Crawls: Instruct the child to practice playing chromatic scales or other scale fragments using a crawling motion, where each finger moves sequentially along the fingerboard. This exercise promotes finger agility, coordination, and speed.

- Trills and Tremolos: Introduce trills and tremolos, which involve rapid alternations between two fingers or quick repetitions of a single note. Guide the child in practicing these

111

techniques gradually, starting at a slow tempo and gradually increasing speed while maintaining accuracy and clarity.

5. Guided Practice Strategies:

   - Slow Practice: Encourage the child to practice exercises and pieces at a slow tempo initially, focusing on finger placement, accuracy, and control. Gradually increase the tempo as the child becomes more comfortable and confident.

   - Finger Warm-Up: Prior to practice sessions, guide the child in performing finger warm-up exercises, such as light finger tapping or finger rolls on a flat surface. This helps loosen up the fingers and prepares them for precise finger movements on the violin.

- Repetition and Consistency: Emphasize the importance of regular practice and repetition to strengthen finger muscles, develop muscle memory, and improve finger dexterity and accuracy. Encourage the child to incorporate specific left hand exercises into their daily practice routine.

6. Musical Application:

- Scale Practice: Incorporate scale exercises into the child's practice routine, focusing on accurate finger placement, consistent finger pressure, and smooth finger transitions. Gradually introduce different scales and key signatures to expand their repertoire of finger patterns.

- Left Hand Etudes: Introduce etudes or studies specifically designed to improve left hand technique. These exercises often contain challenging finger patterns and require precise finger movements. Work on these pieces together, providing guidance and feedback to help the child overcome technical difficulties.

By focusing on left hand exercises for finger dexterity and accuracy, young violinists can enhance their technical skills and perform with greater precision and control. Through consistent practice, patience, and guidance, they will develop the necessary foundation to navigate the fingerboard confidently and expressively.

FINGER PLACEMENT AND SHIFTING

Developing accurate finger placement and smooth shifting is essential for young violinists to navigate the fingerboard with precision and fluidity. Here is an extensive guide on finger placement and shifting tailored for children:

1. Finger Placement:

   - Finger Positioning: Teach the child the correct hand and finger positioning, ensuring that the fingers are curved and the fingertips land precisely on the intended notes. Emphasize the importance of placing the fingers close to the strings without touching

115

adjacent strings, enabling clear and resonant sound production.

- Visual and Tactile Cues: Help the child develop a sense of finger placement by providing visual and tactile cues. Use stickers or tape on the fingerboard to mark specific finger positions, gradually removing them as the child becomes more confident in finger placement.

2. Finger Independence and Mobility:

- Finger Lifts and Drops: Encourage the child to practice lifting and dropping each finger independently on the fingerboard while maintaining the other fingers down. This exercise promotes finger independence, strengthens finger muscles, and improves coordination.

116

- Finger Patterns: Guide the child in practicing finger patterns, such as scales or arpeggios, which involve sequential finger movements. Emphasize accuracy and smooth transitions between fingers to develop fluidity and agility.

3. Shifting:

- Half-Position Shifting: Introduce the concept of half-position shifting, where the hand and fingers move as a unit to a higher or lower position on the fingerboard while maintaining the same finger pattern. Guide the child in practicing simple melodies or exercises that require shifting within a limited range, gradually expanding the shifting range as they gain proficiency.

- Listening and Aural Awareness: Encourage the child to develop a keen sense of pitch and aural awareness when shifting positions. Help them listen attentively to the target note and aim for accurate intonation while shifting.

  - Sliding Technique: Teach the child the sliding technique for smooth and seamless shifting. Instruct them to maintain a relaxed hand and forearm while sliding the fingers along the fingerboard, ensuring that the sound remains continuous and uninterrupted during the shift.

4. Guided Practice Strategies:

  - Slow and Controlled Shifting: Encourage the child to practice shifting at a slow tempo initially, focusing on accuracy and maintaining a consistent finger pattern throughout the shift. Emphasize the importance of precision

118

over speed during the early stages of shifting practice.

- Shifting Exercises: Incorporate shifting exercises into the child's practice routine. These can include specific shifting patterns or passages from repertoire pieces that require precise shifts. Guide the child in breaking down the shifts into smaller segments, practicing them slowly and gradually increasing the speed and accuracy.

- Visual and Muscle Memory: Help the child develop visual and muscle memory by practicing shifting exercises with visual aids, such as marking the target positions on the fingerboard or using finger guides. This reinforces the connection between the visual cues and the physical finger movements required for accurate shifting.

119

5. Musical Application:

  - Repertoire Selection: Choose repertoire pieces that contain shifting passages suitable for the child's level. Work on these pieces together, focusing on accurate finger placement and smooth shifting. Break down the shifting passages into smaller sections and practice them separately before integrating them into the whole piece.

  - Expressive Shifting: Guide the child in understanding the expressive aspects of shifting. Demonstrate and encourage them to use shifting as a means to shape phrases, create dynamic contrasts, and convey emotions in the music they play.

6. *Patience and Persistence:*

- Shifting can be challenging for young violinists, and it requires patience and persistence to master. Encourage the child to approach shifting practice with a positive mindset, celebrating small improvements and progress along the way. Remind them that consistent and focused practice will lead to greater ease and confidence in shifting over time.

By focusing on finger placement and shifting, young violinists can develop accuracy, fluidity, and expressiveness in their playing. Through consistent practice, guided exercises, and musical application, they will acquire the necessary skills to navigate the fingerboard with precision and

confidence, enhancing their overall
performance on the violin.

FINGER INDEPENDENCE AND STRENGTH

Developing finger independence and strength is crucial for young violinists to navigate the fingerboard with precision, agility, and control. Here is an extensive guide on exercises and techniques to enhance finger independence and strength tailored for children:

1. Finger Lifts and Drops:

- Independent Finger Lifts: Encourage the child to practice lifting and dropping each finger independently on the fingerboard while keeping the other fingers down. This exercise helps develop finger independence and control.

- Finger Drops: Guide the child in practicing finger drops, where they start with all fingers lifted and then drop them onto the fingerboard one by one, ensuring clear and simultaneous contact with the strings. This exercise promotes finger strength and coordination.

2. Finger Tapping and Individual Articulation:

- Finger Tapping: Teach the child to tap each finger individually on the fingerboard, focusing on maintaining the other fingers in a relaxed position. This exercise helps develop finger strength, control, and precision.

- Articulation Exercises: Guide the child in practicing exercises that require playing separate notes with each finger, emphasizing clear and distinct articulation. Start with simple patterns and gradually increase the complexity, promoting finger independence and accuracy.

3. Finger Stretching and Flexibility:

- Finger Extensions: Help the child develop finger stretching by practicing exercises that involve placing fingers on adjacent strings simultaneously, requiring stretching and flexibility. Guide them in maintaining proper hand and finger positions while comfortably reaching the desired notes.

- Finger Rolls: Instruct the child to perform finger rolls, where they roll each finger from one string to the adjacent string. This exercise promotes finger flexibility, dexterity, and control.

125

4. Finger Strength Exercises:

  - Finger Push-Ups: Demonstrate and guide the child in performing finger push-ups, where each finger is pressed down on the fingerboard one at a time and lifted up again. This exercise helps develop finger strength, control, and endurance.

  - Finger Pressing: Instruct the child to practice pressing down on the strings with each finger, focusing on producing a clear and resonant sound. Encourage them to gradually increase the pressure, building finger strength while maintaining a relaxed hand and arm position.

5. Scales and Finger Patterns:

  - Scale Practice: Incorporate scale exercises into the child's practice routine, emphasizing accurate finger placement and smooth transitions between fingers. Gradually introduce different scales and key signatures to expand their repertoire of finger patterns, promoting finger independence and agility.

- Finger Pattern Exercises: Guide the child in practicing exercises that involve specific finger patterns, such as thirds, fourths, or chromatic passages. Emphasize accuracy, speed, and smooth transitions between fingers to develop finger independence and strength.

6. Etudes and Repertoire:

- Etudes: Introduce etudes or technical studies specifically designed to improve finger independence and strength. These exercises often contain

127

challenging finger patterns and require precise finger movements. Work on these pieces together, providing guidance and feedback to help the child overcome technical difficulties.

   - Repertoire Selection: Choose repertoire pieces that offer opportunities to develop finger independence and strength. Focus on passages that require quick finger changes, string crossings, or challenging finger patterns. Practice these passages separately, gradually integrating them into the whole piece.

7. Patience and Consistency:

   - Developing finger independence and strength takes time and consistent practice. Encourage the child to approach these exercises with patience and persistence, celebrating small improvements along the way. Remind them that regular and focused practice will lead to greater finger control, agility, and strength over time.

By incorporating exercises and techniques that promote finger independence and strength, young violinists can enhance their technical skills and perform with greater precision, agility, and control. With consistent practice, guidance, and a positive mindset, they will develop the necessary foundation to navigate the fingerboard confidently and expressively.

INTRODUCING BASIC MUSIC NOTATION AND READING SKILLS

Learning to read and understand music notation is an essential skill for young musicians. It provides a foundation for musical communication and enables them to interpret and perform music accurately. Here is an extensive guide on introducing basic music notation and reading skills to children:

1. Musical Staff and Clefs:

   - Introduce the Musical Staff: Begin by explaining the concept of the musical staff, consisting of five horizontal lines and four spaces. Teach the child to recognize and identify the lines and spaces on the staff.

- Clefs: Introduce the treble clef (G clef) and bass clef (F clef) as the most commonly used clefs. Explain that the treble clef is used for higher-pitched instruments like the violin and flute, while the bass clef is used for lower-pitched instruments like the cello and double bass.

2. Note Names and Durations:

- Note Names: Teach the child the names of the notes on the lines and spaces of both the treble and bass clefs. Start with the notes that fall within the range of their instrument and gradually expand their knowledge. Use mnemonics such as "Every Good Boy Does Fine" and "FACE" to help them remember note names.

- Note Durations: Introduce the concept of note durations, including

131

whole notes, half notes, quarter notes, and eighth notes. Explain the relationship between these durations and their corresponding rests.

3. Rhythm and Time Signatures:

  - Rhythm Basics: Teach the child the fundamental concepts of rhythm, such as beat, meter, and time signature. Help them understand the relationship between notes and rests in relation to the beat.

  - Time Signatures: Introduce common time signatures like 4/4, ¾, and 2/4. Explain that the top number represents the number of beats per measure, while the bottom number represents the note value representing one beat.

4. Sight-Reading Exercises:

- Simple Melodies: Provide the child with simple melodies written in their instrument's range. Encourage them to identify the notes, rhythms, and any musical symbols present. Guide them in playing these melodies on their instrument while following the notation.

- Gradual Difficulty: Gradually increase the complexity of the sight-reading exercises as the child's reading skills improve. Introduce additional musical symbols such as dynamics, articulations, and key signatures to expand their understanding.

5. Music Theory Concepts:

- Intervals: Teach the child about intervals, the distance between two

133

notes. Explain concepts like steps (seconds), skips (thirds), and octaves. Help them recognize and identify intervals on the staff.

- Key Signatures: Introduce the concept of key signatures and their relationship to scales. Teach them to recognize key signatures and understand their impact on note reading and finger positions.

- Dynamics and Articulations: Introduce basic dynamic markings (e.g., piano, forte) and articulations (e.g., staccato, legato). Explain their meaning and guide the child in incorporating these expressive elements into their playing.

6. Practice Strategies:

- Regular Practice: Encourage the child to practice reading music regularly. Provide them with a variety of reading materials, including sheet music, sight-reading exercises, and music theory workbooks.

- Breaking it Down: Help the child break down complex passages into smaller segments to facilitate learning. Focus on understanding the rhythms, identifying note patterns, and gradually combining them.

- Metronome Use: Incorporate the use of a metronome to develop a strong sense of timing and steady rhythm. Guide the child in playing along with the metronome to improve their accuracy and tempo control.

7. Interactive Learning Tools:

- Music Apps and Games: Utilize interactive music apps and games that offer engaging activities to reinforce music notation and reading skills. These tools can provide a fun and interactive way for children to practice and reinforce their understanding of music notation.

8. Music Theory Lessons:

- Consider enrolling the child in music theory lessons or group classes. These structured lessons can provide a comprehensive understanding of music notation and reading skills under the guidance of an experienced instructor.

136

9. Support and Encouragement:

- Provide continuous support and encouragement to the child as they learn music notation and reading skills. Celebrate their progress, offer constructive feedback, and foster a positive and enjoyable learning environment.

By introducing basic music notation and reading skills to young musicians, they can develop a solid foundation for musical literacy. With consistent practice, exposure to various musical pieces, and a supportive learning environment, children will gain confidence in reading and interpreting music, opening doors to a lifetime of musical exploration and enjoyment.

NOTE NAMES AND VALUES

Learning note names and values is essential for young violinists to read and interpret sheet music accurately. Here is an extensive guide on note names and values tailored for children:

1. Note Names:

- Open Strings: Begin by teaching the child the note names of the open strings on the violin: G, D, A, and E. Explain that each string produces a specific pitch and has its own note name.

- Fingered Notes: Introduce the concept of fingered notes, where the child uses their fingers to produce different pitches on the fingerboard. Teach them the finger placements for

the notes on the D and A strings,
starting with the first and second
fingers.

2. *Note Values:*

   - Whole Note: Introduce the whole
note, which is represented by an open
oval shape. Explain that the whole note
receives four beats in 4/4 time.

   - Half Note: Teach the concept of the
half note, represented by an open oval
with a stem. Explain that the half note
receives two beats in 4/4 time.

   - Quarter Note: Introduce the
quarter note, represented by a filled-in
oval with a stem. Explain that the
quarter note receives one beat in 4/4
time.

   - Eighth Note: Teach the concept of
the eighth note, represented by a

filled-in oval with a stem and a flag. Explain that the eighth note receives half a beat in 4/4 time.

3. *Note Duration and Counting:*

- Whole Note: Help the child understand that a whole note lasts for four beats. Practice counting aloud while clapping or tapping along to internalize the concept of duration.

- Half Note: Explain that a half note lasts for two beats. Guide the child in counting and playing rhythms that incorporate half notes.

- Quarter Note: Introduce the concept of a quarter note lasting for one beat. Encourage the child to count and play rhythms that consist of quarter notes.

- Eighth Note: Teach the child that an eighth note lasts for half a beat. Demonstrate and practice counting and playing rhythms that include eighth notes.

4. *Note Reading Exercises:*

- Simple Melodies: Provide the child with sheet music containing simple melodies within their playing range. Encourage them to identify the note names and their corresponding finger placements. Guide them in playing these melodies while focusing on note values and rhythm accuracy.

- Sight-Reading: Gradually introduce sight-reading exercises that incorporate a variety of note names and values. Start with simple exercises and progress to more complex ones as the child's reading skills improve.

141

Emphasize accuracy and fluency in both note identification and rhythm execution.

5. Flashcards and Games:

  - Note Flashcards: Create or use note flashcards to help the child associate note names with their positions on the staff. Practice identifying and saying the names of the notes quickly and accurately.

  - Music Note Games: Engage the child in interactive music note games and apps that reinforce note names and values. These games can make the learning process enjoyable and engaging.

142

6. Repertoire Selection:

- Choose repertoire pieces that gradually introduce new notes and rhythms. Select pieces with simple melodies and rhythms at first, and progress to more complex compositions as the child becomes more proficient in note reading and rhythm execution.

- Encourage the child to practice these pieces regularly, focusing on accurate note placement and rhythm adherence.

7. Regular Practice and Reinforcement:

- Emphasize the importance of regular practice to reinforce note names and values. Encourage the child to spend dedicated time each day

143

reviewing and practicing note identification and rhythm exercises.

   - Incorporate note-reading exercises and rhythm drills into their practice routine to strengthen their skills systematically.

8. Patience and Progress:

   - Learning note names and values takes time and consistent effort. Encourage the child to be patient with themselves and celebrate their progress along the way. Remind them that with regular practice, their note reading skills will improve steadily.

By introducing note names and values to young violinists in a systematic and engaging manner, they will gradually develop the ability to read and

144

interpret sheet music accurately. With consistent practice, guidance, and a positive attitude, children can become proficient in identifying note names and durations, enhancing their overall musicianship and enjoyment of playing the violin.

READING SIMPLE MELODIES

Learning to read and play simple melodies is an exciting milestone for young violinists. It allows them to apply their knowledge of note names, rhythms, and finger placements to perform music. Here is an extensive guide on reading simple melodies specifically designed for children:

1. Mastering Note Names:

- Review Note Names: Begin by reinforcing the knowledge of note names on the staff, including open string notes (G, D, A, E) and fingered notes on the D and A strings.

- Associating Notes with Finger Placements: Help the child associate specific note names with the corresponding finger placements on the fingerboard. Practice identifying and playing notes with different fingerings.

2. Understanding Rhythms:

- Note Durations: Review note durations such as whole notes, half notes, quarter notes, and eighth notes. Ensure the child understands the relationship between these note values and their corresponding durations.

- Clapping and Counting: Engage the child in clapping or tapping exercises while counting the beats to internalize the rhythmic patterns. Encourage them to associate the note durations with the appropriate number of beats.

3. Identifying Melodic Patterns:

- Stepwise Motion: Introduce simple melodies that primarily move in stepwise motion (consecutive notes on the staff). Guide the child to recognize and play these patterns on their violin.

- Repeated Patterns: Help the child identify repeated melodic patterns within a piece. Emphasize the importance of recognizing these patterns as they simplify the learning process.

4. Sight-Reading Exercises:

- Gradual Difficulty: Provide the child with easy sight-reading exercises that consist of simple melodies within their playing range. Start with exercises that focus on stepwise motion and gradually introduce small leaps.

- Familiarization with Key Signatures: Introduce basic key signatures, such as G major (one sharp) and D major (two sharps). Help the child become familiar with these key signatures and how they affect note reading on the staff.

5. Visualizing Finger Placements:

- Fingerboard Mapping: Encourage the child to visualize the finger placements on the fingerboard while reading the notes on the staff. Guide them to associate specific fingerings with the corresponding notes.

- Fingerboard Markers: Consider using temporary fingerboard markers (e.g., stickers or tape) to assist the child in locating the correct finger placements for notes. Gradually

149

remove the markers as their finger
awareness improves.

6. Repertoire Selection:

- Choose Simple Melodies: Select
repertoire pieces that feature simple,
well-known melodies suitable for
beginners. Look for compositions with
clear note progressions and repetitive
patterns.

- Familiar Songs: Introduce familiar
songs or nursery rhymes that the child
can connect with. Playing melodies
they already know can enhance their
motivation and engagement in the
learning process.

7. Emphasizing Accuracy and Expression:

- Accuracy: Encourage the child to focus on accurate intonation and finger placements while playing simple melodies. Guide them to pay attention to pitch and develop a sense of correct finger position.

- Expression: Teach the child to incorporate basic dynamics (e.g., piano, forte) and articulations (e.g., staccato, legato) to add expression to their playing. Help them understand how these markings affect the interpretation of the melody.

8. Regular Practice and Progress Tracking:

- Establish a Practice Routine: Encourage the child to practice reading

151

simple melodies regularly. Set specific goals for each practice session and track their progress over time.

   - Record and Review: Encourage the child to record themselves playing the melodies and listen back for self-assessment. This helps them identify areas for improvement and provides a sense of accomplishment as they observe their progress.

9. *Support and Encouragement:*

   - Provide continuous support and encouragement to the child as they read and play simple melodies. Celebrate their achievements, offer constructive feedback, and foster a positive and nurturing learning environment.

By following this comprehensive guide, young violinists can develop the skills necessary to read and perform simple melodies with confidence. With consistent practice, guidance, and a love for music, children will continue to explore and expand their repertoire, paving the way for their musical growth and enjoyment on the violin.

BUILDING REPERTOIRE

Building a repertoire is an essential aspect of musical development for any musician, including young violinists. It involves learning and mastering a collection of songs and pieces that showcase different styles, techniques, and musical concepts. Here is an extensive guide on building repertoire tailored for children:

1. Selection of Repertoire:

- Varied Styles: Choose repertoire that represents a variety of musical styles and genres, including classical, folk, and popular music. This exposes the child to different musical expressions and fosters versatility.

- Progressive Difficulty: Select pieces that gradually increase in difficulty to ensure a continuous challenge and growth in the child's playing abilities. Start with simpler melodies and progress towards more complex compositions.

- Age-Appropriate Content: Consider the child's age and musical maturity when selecting repertoire. Opt for pieces that resonate with their interests and are suitable for their technical and emotional development.

2. Establishing Goals:

- Short-Term and Long-Term Goals: Set both short-term and long-term goals with the child. Short-term goals can be focused on mastering specific techniques or sections of a piece, while long-term goals can involve performing in recitals or competitions.

   - Balancing Difficulty: Strike a balance between challenging repertoire that pushes the child's boundaries and more accessible pieces that allow for a sense of accomplishment. This helps maintain motivation and confidence.

3. Breakdown and Analysis:

   - Structural Analysis: Help the child understand the structure of each piece by identifying sections, repeats, and variations. This analysis enhances their overall comprehension and interpretation of the music.

   - Melodic and Harmonic Analysis: Discuss the melodic and harmonic elements present in the piece. Encourage the child to identify key changes, chord progressions, and melodic motifs, fostering a deeper understanding of the music.

4. Learning Strategies:

- Sectional Practice: Break down the piece into smaller sections and work on each section separately. This approach allows the child to focus on specific technical challenges and gradually integrate them into the whole piece.

- Slow Practice: Encourage the child to practice difficult passages at a slower tempo, focusing on accuracy, intonation, and expression. As they gain proficiency, gradually increase the tempo.

- Practice Techniques: Introduce various practice techniques, such as scales, arpeggios, and technical

157

exercises, that directly address the technical demands of the repertoire. This strengthens the child's technical foundation and facilitates smoother execution of the pieces.

5. Interpretation and Expression:

   - Musical Interpretation: Guide the child in developing their own interpretation of the repertoire. Encourage them to experiment with dynamics, phrasing, and articulation to bring out the expressive qualities of the music.

   - Emotional Connection: Help the child connect emotionally with the repertoire by encouraging them to explore the story or mood behind each piece. This fosters a deeper level of musical expression and engagement.

6. Performance Opportunities:

- Recitals and Competitions: Encourage the child to participate in recitals, competitions, or school concerts to gain performance experience. These opportunities promote confidence, stage presence, and a sense of achievement.

- Informal Settings: Create informal performance opportunities at home, such as family gatherings or small recitals with fellow musicians. This helps the child develop comfort and ease in front of an audience.

7. Recording and Self-Assessment:

- Recordings: Encourage the child to record themselves playing pieces from their repertoire. Listening to these recordings allows them to objectively assess their playing, identify areas for improvement, and track their progress over time.

- Self-Assessment: Teach the child to critically evaluate their own performances by listening for intonation, tone quality, dynamics, and overall musicality. This cultivates a sense of musical independence and self-reflection.

8. Continuous Learning:

- Expanding Repertoire: Continuously add new songs and pieces to the repertoire. This broadens the child's musical horizons, exposes them to different composers and styles, and encourages lifelong learning.

160

- Technical and Musical Challenges: Introduce repertoire that specifically targets technical or musical challenges the child may encounter. This ensures a well-rounded development and a constant push towards improvement.

9. *Guidance and Support:*

- Teacher Involvement: Collaborate closely with the child's music teacher to receive guidance, feedback, and suggestions for repertoire selection. The teacher's expertise and experience are invaluable in the child's musical journey.

- Encouragement and Motivation: Provide ongoing support, encouragement, and praise to inspire the child's passion for music and their dedication to building a repertoire.

161

Celebrate their achievements, both big and small.

By following this comprehensive guide, young violinists can effectively build and expand their repertoire. Through careful repertoire selection, setting goals, focused practice, and performance opportunities, children can cultivate a diverse musical palette, enhance their technical skills, and develop their musicality. This process not only nurtures their love for music but also prepares them for future musical endeavors and a lifelong appreciation of the violin.

BEGINNER-LEVEL SONGS

For young children starting their journey as violinists, beginner-level songs play a crucial role in developing their skills and nurturing their love for music. These songs are carefully selected to suit their technical abilities and musical understanding. Here is an extensive collection of beginner-level songs specifically designed for children violinists:

1. "Twinkle, Twinkle, Little Star":

- This beloved nursery rhyme is a perfect starting point for young violinists. Its simple melody and repetitive structure make it easy to learn and remember. Focus on playing it with clear intonation and a gentle, flowing bowing technique.

2. *"Mary Had a Little Lamb"*:

   - Another classic nursery rhyme, "Mary Had a Little Lamb" is an excellent choice for beginners. Its familiar melody helps children develop their ear training and pitch recognition. Encourage them to add expressive touches, such as dynamics and phrasing.

3. *"Hot Cross Buns"*:

   - "Hot Cross Buns" is a catchy folk song that introduces young violinists to basic finger patterns. Its repetitive nature allows children to focus on finger placement and coordination.

164

Emphasize clear and accurate note production.

4. "Merrily We Roll Along":

   - This cheerful folk tune is an ideal song for developing bowing technique and coordination. Encourage the child to play with a smooth, even bow stroke and pay attention to dynamics to bring out the lively character of the melody.

5. "Go Tell Aunt Rhody":

   - "Go Tell Aunt Rhody" is a traditional folk song that provides an opportunity for young violinists to practice simple melodies with varying rhythms. Help the child understand

165

and execute the different note durations accurately.

6. "Ode to Joy":

 - The famous melody from Beethoven's Ninth Symphony, "Ode to Joy," is an excellent introduction to playing classical music. Start with a simplified version and gradually incorporate more advanced techniques such as slurs and dynamics.

7. "Jingle Bells":

 - A holiday favorite, "Jingle Bells" is a festive song that children enjoy playing. It introduces them to more complex rhythms and requires coordination between fingerings and bowing. Encourage them to capture the joyful spirit of the piece.

8. "London Bridge Is Falling Down":

- "London Bridge Is Falling Down" is a traditional nursery rhyme with a memorable melody. It provides an opportunity for young violinists to practice playing in different positions on the violin. Guide them through the finger placements and shifts.

9. "Can Can":

- The lively and energetic "Can Can" by Jacques Offenbach is a fun piece that introduces children to faster tempo and more challenging bowing techniques. Break it down into

167

manageable sections and gradually increase the tempo as their skills progress.

10. *"Au Clair de la Lune":*

   - This French folk song offers a beautiful and melodic piece for young violinists. It focuses on playing legato and developing a smooth bowing technique. Encourage the child to bring out the expressive qualities of the melody.

11. *"When the Saints Go Marching In":*

   - "When the Saints Go Marching In" is a catchy tune that introduces children to syncopated rhythms and finger patterns. Emphasize a lively and upbeat playing style while maintaining accurate note placement.

12. "Skip to My Lou":

- "Skip to My Lou" is a playful American folk song that helps children develop their sense of rhythm and coordination between bowing and fingering. Encourage them to experiment with dynamics and explore different bowing techniques.

Remember, the key to successful learning is to break down these songs into smaller sections, practice them regularly, and gradually increase the difficulty as the child progresses. Celebrate their achievements and provide a supportive and encouraging learning environment. With this

169

delightful repertoire of beginner-level songs, young violinists can embark on a fulfilling musical journey filled with joy, growth, and a lifelong love for the violin.

INTERMEDIATE-LEVEL PIECES

As young violinists progress in their musical journey, intermediate-level songs play a vital role in further developing their technical skills and musical understanding. These songs offer increased complexity and musical depth, providing opportunities for growth and artistic expression. Here is an extensive collection of intermediate-level songs specifically curated for children violinists:

1. "Minuet in G" by Johann Sebastian Bach:

- Bach's "Minuet in G" is a delightful piece that introduces young violinists to Baroque music. It challenges them with more intricate fingerings, bowing techniques, and phrasing. Emphasize clarity, precision, and a sense of elegance in their performance.

2. "Gavotte" by Francois-Joseph Gossec:

- Gossec's "Gavotte" is a lively and rhythmic piece that showcases the child's bowing dexterity and control. Encourage them to articulate the distinct character of each section, from the stately opening to the spirited dance-like passages.

3. "Sonatina in G Major" by Ludwig van Beethoven:

- Beethoven's "Sonatina in G Major" offers a taste of classical sonata form. This piece challenges young violinists with its melodic lines, varied dynamics, and shifting moods. Help them navigate the contrasting sections and maintain a cohesive interpretation.

4. "Meditation" from Thaïs by Jules Massenet:

- The beautiful and lyrical "Meditation" from Massenet's opera Thaïs is an opportunity for young violinists to explore expressive playing. Guide them in shaping phrases, using vibrato tastefully, and portraying the emotional depth of the piece.

5. "Humoresque" by Antonin Dvořák:

- Dvořák's "Humoresque" is a charming and playful piece that allows young violinists to showcase their technical skills. It requires precise fingerwork, bow control for staccato passages, and a sense of rhythmic vitality.

6. "Sicilienne" by Maria Theresia von Paradis:

   - Paradis' "Sicilienne" is a lyrical and introspective composition that encourages young violinists to focus on tone production and expressive phrasing. Help them bring out the song-like qualities of the melody while maintaining a balanced tone.

7. "The Swan" from Carnival of the Animals by Camille Saint-Saëns:

   - Saint-Saëns' "The Swan" is a beautiful and melancholic piece that allows young violinists to explore legato playing and expressive techniques such as portamento. Encourage them to convey the graceful and serene nature of the swan's movements.

8. "Czardas" by Vittorio Monti:

- Monti's "Czardas" is a fiery and virtuosic piece that challenges young violinists with its fast tempo, shifting rhythms, and technical passages. Guide them in maintaining clarity and precision while infusing the piece with energy and passion.

9. "Serenade" by Joseph Haydn:

- Haydn's "Serenade" is a delightful and elegant piece that allows young

175

violinists to explore graceful phrasing and dynamic contrasts. Encourage them to bring out the charming character of the serenade through nuanced playing.

10. "Rondo" from Abdelazer by Henry Purcell:

- Purcell's "Rondo" is a lively and spirited piece that showcases young violinists' technical agility and bowing control. Focus on maintaining a steady tempo, articulating the rhythmic patterns, and conveying the exuberant nature of the music.

11. "Romance" by Carl Maria von Weber:

- Weber's "Romance" is a lyrical and expressive composition that offers young violinists an opportunity to develop their musicality and phrasing. Guide them in shaping long, singing lines and capturing the emotional nuances of the piece.

12. "Danse Macabre" by Camille Saint-Saëns:

- Saint-Saëns' "Danse Macabre" is a thrilling and dramatic piece that allows young violinists to explore a wide range of techniques, including double stops, rapid bowing, and dynamic contrasts. Help them create a vivid and haunting interpretation.

As young violinists tackle these intermediate-level songs, encourage them to embrace the challenges and express their musicality. Focus on refining technical skills, developing a nuanced interpretation, and fostering a deep connection with the music. With these captivating and diverse repertoire choices, young violinists can continue to expand their musical horizons and embark on a rewarding musical journey.

ADVANCED-LEVEL REPERTOIRE

For young violinists who have reached an advanced level of proficiency, exploring a diverse and challenging repertoire is essential for their continued growth and artistic development. Advanced-level pieces for children violinists offer opportunities to showcase technical mastery, musical expressiveness, and a deep understanding of musical interpretation. Here is an extensive collection of advanced-level repertoire specifically curated for young violinists:

179

1. "Mozart Violin Concerto No. 3 in G Major":

- Mozart's Violin Concerto No. 3 is a masterpiece of the violin repertoire. It presents technical challenges such as rapid scale passages, double stops, and intricate bowing techniques. Encourage the young violinist to delve into the nuances of Mozart's music, showcasing a balance between technical precision and lyrical expression.

2. "Introduction and Rondo Capriccioso" by Camille Saint-Saëns:

- Saint-Saëns' "Introduction and Rondo Capriccioso" is a virtuosic showpiece that demands technical brilliance and agility. The piece showcases rapid bowing, double stops, harmonics, and advanced fingerings. Encourage the young violinist to unleash their musicality and captivate the audience with their technical prowess.

3. "Zigeunerweisen" by Pablo de Sarasate:

  - "Zigeunerweisen" by Sarasate is a thrilling and fiery composition that challenges young violinists with its demanding technical passages, including rapid scale runs, double stops, and extended techniques. Guide the young violinist to bring out the passionate and expressive nature of the piece.

181

4. "Carmen Fantasy" by Pablo de Sarasate:

   - Sarasate's "Carmen Fantasy" is a dazzling display of virtuosity, combining themes from Bizet's opera "Carmen" with elaborate variations and technical fireworks. Encourage the young violinist to convey the dramatic character of the music, emphasizing precision, agility, and expressive phrasing.

5. "Symphonie Espagnole" by Édouard Lalo:

   - Lalo's "Symphonie Espagnole" is a challenging and captivating work for advanced young violinists. It showcases a wide range of technical demands, including rapid passages, double stops, and intricate bowing

182

patterns. Guide the young violinist to explore the Spanish-inspired melodies and bring out the vibrant colors of the music.

6. "Violin Concerto in D Major" by Pyotr Ilyich Tchaikovsky:

- Tchaikovsky's Violin Concerto in D Major is a monumental work that demands technical brilliance and emotional depth. It features soaring melodies, intricate passages, and powerful virtuosic sections. Encourage the young violinist to master the technical challenges while conveying the intense emotional journey of the concerto.

7. "Caprice No. 24" by Niccolò Paganini:

- Paganini's "Caprice No. 24" is a legendary piece known for its technical complexity and brilliance. It requires advanced bowing techniques, left-hand agility, and precise articulation. Guide the young violinist to showcase their technical mastery and interpret the piece with flair and virtuosity.

8. "Violin Sonata No. 9 in A Major" by Ludwig van Beethoven:

- Beethoven's Violin Sonata No. 9, also known as the "Kreutzer Sonata," is a monumental work requiring advanced technical skills and interpretive maturity. It demands mastery of intricate passages, expressiveness, and a deep

184

understanding of the composer's
intentions.

9. "Bruch Violin Concerto No. 1 in G Minor":

- Bruch's Violin Concerto No. 1 is a beloved concerto that showcases the expressive capabilities of the violin. It features beautiful melodies, demanding technical passages, and opportunities for the young violinist to demonstrate their lyrical phrasing and emotional depth.

10. "Praeludium and Allegro" by Fritz Kreisler:

- Kreisler's "Praeludium and Allegro" is a charming and virtuosic piece that demands advanced bowing techniques,

185

double stops, and intricate fingerwork. Encourage the young violinist to bring out the elegance and gracefulness of the piece while maintaining technical brilliance.

When working on advanced-level repertoire, it is crucial to encourage young violinists to approach the pieces with discipline, patience, and a commitment to musical excellence. Guide them in mastering the technical challenges while nurturing their artistic expression and interpretation. With these advanced-level pieces, young violinists can continue to elevate their skills, captivate audiences, and embark on a remarkable musical journey.

DEVELOPING EAR TRAINING AND INTONATION SKILLS

Ear training and intonation are crucial aspects of violin playing that greatly contribute to a young musician's overall musicality and precision. Developing a keen ear and honing intonation skills not only enhance a violinist's ability to play in tune but also facilitate musical expression and ensemble playing. Here are some effective strategies and exercises to help children violinists develop their ear training and intonation skills:

1. Singing and Pitch Matching:

- Encourage young violinists to sing the pitches they are about to play before playing them on the violin. This helps them internalize the pitch and develop a strong connection between their ear and their fingers. Practice pitch matching exercises where the child sings a note, and then plays it on the violin, comparing the pitch accuracy.

2. Tuning with Open Strings:

   - Have the child practice tuning their violin using open strings as reference pitches. Help them develop the ability to listen carefully and make small adjustments to match the pitch of the reference string. Encourage them to focus on the differences in sound and make incremental adjustments until the pitches align.

188

3. Interval Recognition:

- Train the young violinist's ear to recognize various intervals by playing them on the piano or another instrument and having the child identify them. Start with simple intervals like seconds and thirds and gradually progress to more complex intervals. This exercise helps develop their ability to hear the distance between notes accurately.

4. Melodic and Harmonic Dictation:

- Engage the child in melodic and harmonic dictation exercises. Play short melodies or chord progressions on the piano or another instrument, and have the child notate the pitches or reproduce them on the violin. This exercise sharpens their listening skills,

189

improves pitch memory, and reinforces their understanding of melodic and harmonic relationships.

5. Playing in Unison or Octaves:

   - Play simple melodies or scales together with the child, either in unison or octaves. Encourage them to listen carefully and match their pitch precisely with yours. This exercise helps develop their ability to play in tune with others and improves their sense of pitch accuracy.

6. Intonation Exercises with Drones:

   - Use drones (sustained pitches) as a reference while the child plays scales, arpeggios, or exercises. The sustained pitch provides a constant reference point for intonation. Encourage the child to listen for the beats or vibrations that occur when their pitch is not perfectly in tune with the drone, and make adjustments accordingly.

7. Listening to Recordings:

- Expose the young violinist to recordings of accomplished violinists performing various pieces. Encourage them to listen attentively to the intonation and nuances in the performances. Discuss the importance of accurate intonation and how it contributes to the overall musical expression.

8. Ensemble Playing:

- Provide opportunities for the child to play in ensemble settings, such as duets or chamber groups. Playing with others requires careful listening and precise intonation to ensure a harmonious blend. This experience helps the child develop their intonation skills in a collaborative musical context.

9. Intonation Exercises within Repertoire:

- Incorporate specific intonation exercises within the child's repertoire. Identify challenging passages or intervals that require extra attention, and have the child practice them slowly and meticulously. Use tools like finger patterns, visual aids, or finger tapes to assist in developing muscle memory and reinforcing correct finger placement.

10. Regular Intonation Checks:

   - During practice sessions, periodically pause and have the child play open strings or simple exercises to check their intonation. This helps them develop a constant awareness of pitch accuracy and allows for immediate corrections if necessary.

Consistency, patience, and regular practice are key to developing ear training and intonation skills. Encourage the child to embrace these exercises as an integral part of their musical journey, as they lay the foundation for precision,

193

expressiveness, and musical excellence
on the violin.

TUNING THE VIOLIN

Ensuring the violin is in tune is a fundamental aspect of playing the instrument. For young violinists, learning to tune their instrument accurately is an essential skill that establishes a solid foundation for their musical journey. Here is a comprehensive guide on tuning the violin specifically tailored for children violinists:

1. Understanding the Strings:

   - Introduce the child to the four strings of the violin: G (thickest), D, A, and E (thinnest). Teach them to identify the strings by their thickness and order.

195

2. Using a Tuning Device:

  - Provide the child with a reliable electronic tuner or a tuner app on a smartphone or tablet. Demonstrate how to use the tuner, explaining that it detects the pitch and indicates whether the string is too high (sharp) or too low (flat).

3. Fine-Tuning Pegs:

  - Show the child how to use the fine-tuning pegs located at the top of the violin's scroll. Explain that small adjustments to the pegs can raise or lower the pitch of each string.

4. Tuning Procedure:

- Guide the child through the step-by-step process of tuning the violin:

a. Start with the A string: Pluck the string gently while watching the tuner. If the tuner indicates the pitch is too high (sharp), turn the peg slightly counterclockwise to lower the pitch. If it's too low (flat), turn the peg slightly clockwise to raise the pitch. Continue adjusting until the tuner shows the correct pitch.

b. Once the A string is in tune, use it as a reference to tune the other strings. Press the finger down on the A string to produce the correct pitch and match it with the open D string. Adjust the D string using the fine-tuning pegs until both strings produce the same pitch. Repeat this process to tune the G and E strings, using the previously tuned strings as references.

197

c. After tuning all the strings, play each string individually to confirm that they are in tune and match the pitches indicated by the tuner.

5. Tuning with a Reference Pitch:

- Teach the child to tune the violin using a reference pitch, such as a tuning fork, piano, or another instrument. Play the reference pitch and have the child match the pitch by adjusting the fine-tuning pegs. This exercise helps the child develop their ear and the ability to tune their instrument without relying solely on electronic tuners.

6. Checking the Intonation:

- Emphasize the importance of checking the intonation of open strings and different finger positions. Encourage the child to listen carefully and make small adjustments using the fine-tuning pegs or finger positions to ensure each note is in tune.

7. Regular Tuning Routine:

- Develop a habit of tuning the violin at the beginning of each practice session. Reinforce the idea that playing an in-tune instrument enhances the quality of sound and overall musical experience.

8. Seeking Assistance:

- Remind the child to seek help from a teacher, parent, or more experienced musician if they encounter difficulties or are unsure about tuning their violin. It is essential to address any issues promptly to maintain proper intonation.

9. Maintenance and Care:

- Teach the child to take care of their instrument by avoiding extreme temperatures, keeping it clean, and periodically checking the strings for wear and tear. Well-maintained strings contribute to better tuning stability.

10. Developing a Musical Ear:

- Encourage the child to listen to well-tuned music regularly, whether through recordings or live performances. This exposure to accurately pitched music helps develop their musical ear and fosters an appreciation for intonation.

By patiently guiding young violinists through the process of tuning their instrument, we provide them with the necessary tools to achieve pitch perfection. With regular practice and a keen ear, children violinists can develop a strong sense of intonation, setting the stage for musical growth and a rewarding violin-playing experience.

PITCH RECOGNITION AND MATCHING

Pitch recognition and matching are vital skills for young violinists, as they enable accurate intonation and harmonious playing. Developing a keen ear and the ability to identify and reproduce pitches on the violin lays the foundation for musical excellence. Here is an extensive guide on pitch recognition and matching specifically designed for children violinists:

1. Listening Exercises:

- Encourage the child to actively listen to a variety of musical pieces, paying attention to the pitches played by different instruments. Discuss the differences in pitch between

202

instruments and help them distinguish high and low pitches, as well as changes in pitch.

2. Singing and Vocalization:

   - Incorporate singing exercises into the child's practice routine. Encourage them to sing the pitches they are about to play on the violin, focusing on accuracy and matching the pitch with their voice. This exercise helps internalize pitch relationships and strengthens the connection between their ear and fingers.

3. Relative Pitch Training:

   - Introduce the concept of relative pitch by teaching the child to identify intervals (the distance between two pitches). Start with simple intervals, such as seconds or thirds, and progress to more complex ones. Use familiar melodies or popular tunes as examples, and have the child identify the intervals by ear.

4. Pitch Memory Games:

- Engage the child in pitch memory games to enhance their ability to remember and reproduce pitches. Play a series of random notes or short melodies on the piano or another instrument, and have the child reproduce them on the violin. Gradually increase the difficulty by introducing longer sequences or more complex melodies.

5. Pitch Matching Exercises:

   - Play a single note on the piano or another instrument and have the child match the pitch by playing the corresponding note on the violin. Start with simple melodies or scales, and gradually progress to more challenging exercises. Emphasize the importance of careful listening and precise reproduction of the pitch.

6. Call and Response:

   - Establish a call-and-response practice routine where you play a short phrase or sequence of notes on the violin, and the child repeats it back accurately. This exercise develops the child's ability to listen attentively, recognize pitch patterns, and reproduce them on their instrument.

205

7. Tuning with a Reference Pitch:

- Teach the child to tune their violin using a reference pitch, such as a tuning fork, piano, or another instrument. Explain the concept of matching the pitch of open strings with the reference pitch and guide them through the process of adjusting the fine-tuning pegs to achieve precise tuning.

8. Playing in Unison:

- Engage in duets or ensemble playing with the child, where you play a simple melody or piece together. Encourage them to listen carefully and match their pitch with yours, aiming for a harmonious blend. This exercise develops their ability to play in tune

with others and reinforces pitch
recognition and matching skills.

9. Melodic Dictation:

  - Play short melodies or sequences
of notes on the piano or another
instrument, and have the child notate
or reproduce them on the violin. This
exercise improves their ability to
recognize and reproduce pitches
accurately, enhancing both their ear
training and music notation skills.

10. Regular Pitch Checks:

  - Incorporate regular pitch checks
during practice sessions. Pause and
have the child play open strings or
simple exercises to assess their pitch
accuracy. Provide guidance and

207

feedback to help them make adjustments when needed.

Consistency and patience are key when developing pitch recognition and matching skills. Encourage the child to embrace these exercises as an exciting part of their musical journey. With regular practice and a focus on attentive listening, young violinists can develop a discerning ear, impeccable intonation, and the ability to create harmonious music on their instrument.

PLAYING IN TUNE WITH OTHERS

Playing in tune with others is a crucial skill for young violinists, as it allows them to create harmonious music within an ensemble or group setting. Developing the ability to listen attentively, adjust pitch, and blend with fellow musicians enhances the overall musical experience. Here is an extensive guide on playing in tune with others specifically tailored for children violinists:

1. Active Listening:

- Emphasize the importance of active listening during ensemble rehearsals or group performances. Encourage the child to pay attention to the music

209

being played around them, focusing on the pitch relationships between different instruments or voices.

2. Tuning as a Group:

   - Teach the child the process of tuning their instrument in a group setting. Explain how each member of the ensemble should tune their instrument using a reference pitch, such as a tuning fork or piano, to ensure everyone starts on the same pitch. Demonstrate the importance of matching the reference pitch accurately to achieve cohesion.

3. Unison Playing:

   - Begin ensemble rehearsals with simple unison exercises where all members play the same melody or piece together. Encourage the child to listen carefully to the group's collective sound and adjust their pitch to match that of their fellow musicians. Highlight the importance of blending and striving for a unified sound.

4. Call and Response:

- Engage in call and response exercises within the ensemble. Take turns playing short phrases or musical fragments, and have the child respond by reproducing the same material accurately. This exercise sharpens their listening skills, promotes pitch matching, and fosters a sense of musical dialogue between performers.

5. Pitch Matching Games:

- Play pitch matching games within the ensemble, where one member plays a pitch or short melody, and the child must reproduce it on their violin. Rotate roles to ensure everyone gets a chance to lead and follow. These games improve the child's ability to recognize and replicate pitches, promoting accuracy in ensemble playing.

6. Playing Alongside a Tuned Instrument:

- Pair the child with a more experienced musician or teacher who plays a tuned instrument, such as a piano or guitar. Have the child play their violin alongside the tuned instrument, focusing on matching their

212

pitch and adjusting when necessary. This exercise helps develop the child's ability to play in tune with others.

7. Intonation Exercises:

- Incorporate intonation exercises into ensemble rehearsals. Practice playing scales, arpeggios, or simple melodies together, with a specific focus on maintaining accurate intonation. Encourage the child to listen carefully to their own playing as well as the ensemble's sound, making adjustments to pitch as needed.

8. Ensemble Dynamics:

- Teach the child the importance of dynamics within an ensemble. Explain how changes in volume and expression

213

can impact the overall sound.
Encourage them to listen to the
ensemble's dynamics and adjust their
playing to match, ensuring a balanced
and cohesive performance.

9. Record and Evaluate:

- Record ensemble rehearsals or
performances and listen back as a
group. Discuss areas where pitch
discrepancies or intonation issues
arise. Encourage constructive feedback
and problem-solving to address these
challenges collectively. This process
helps the child develop a critical ear
and promotes collaborative learning.

10. Performances and Collaborations:

- Provide opportunities for the child to participate in performances and collaborations with other musicians. Whether it's playing in a school orchestra, chamber group, or ensemble, these experiences foster the child's ability to play in tune with others, adapt to different musical styles, and contribute to a unified musical performance.

By nurturing their listening skills, promoting pitch awareness, and fostering a sense of musical unity, young violinists can develop the ability to play in tune with others. Encourage them to embrace the collaborative nature of ensemble playing, as it not only enriches their musical growth but

215

also nurtures a deeper appreciation for
the beauty of harmonious music.

PRACTICING TECHNIQUES AND CREATING EFFECTIVE PRACTICE ROUTINES

Developing good practicing techniques and establishing effective practice routines is essential for the growth and progress of young violinists. By incorporating focused and structured practice sessions, children can maximize their learning potential and achieve musical excellence. Here is an extensive guide on practicing techniques and creating effective practice routines specifically designed for children violinists:

1. Set Clear Goals:

   - Begin each practice session by setting clear and achievable goals.

217

Discuss with the child what they aim to accomplish, whether it's mastering a specific piece, improving a challenging passage, or enhancing overall technique. Setting goals provides direction and motivation.

2. Warm-Up Exercises:

  - Start with warm-up exercises to prepare the body and mind for practice. Incorporate activities such as stretching, gentle finger exercises, and bowing exercises to loosen up muscles and improve flexibility. This helps prevent injuries and enhances technical accuracy.

3. Break It Down:

- Break down challenging pieces or passages into smaller sections. Focus on one section at a time, working on intonation, rhythm, and expression. Practice slowly and gradually increase the tempo as proficiency improves. This approach promotes accuracy and prevents frustration.

4. Repetition and Muscle Memory:

- Emphasize repetition as a means of developing muscle memory. Encourage the child to repeat challenging sections multiple times, ensuring consistent finger placement, bowing technique, and intonation. Repetition strengthens neural connections and facilitates automaticity.

5. Attention to Detail:

   - Encourage the child to pay attention to details. Focus on articulation, dynamics, phrasing, and tone quality. Guide them to listen critically to their own playing and make adjustments accordingly. Attention to detail enhances musicality and expression.

6. Slow Practice:

   - Incorporate slow practice into the routine. Slow tempo allows for careful analysis of technique, intonation, and bow control. It promotes precision and enables the child to identify and correct errors or weaknesses.

7. Practice with a Metronome:

  - Introduce the use of a metronome during practice sessions. Practicing with a steady beat improves rhythm, timing, and coordination. Start at a comfortable tempo and gradually increase the speed as proficiency improves.

8. Sight-Reading:

  - Include sight-reading exercises in practice routines. Provide the child with new and unfamiliar music to sight-read. This improves reading skills, rhythm comprehension, and adaptability to different musical styles.

221

9. Ear Training:

  - Dedicate time to ear training exercises. Practice playing melodies by ear, identifying intervals, and replicating pitches on the violin. This enhances the child's ability to recognize and reproduce pitches accurately.

10. Practice Variations:

  - Incorporate practice variations to maintain engagement and prevent monotony. This can include playing a piece in different tempos, dynamics, or bowing styles. It encourages adaptability and creativity.

11. Recording and Self-Evaluation:

- Encourage the child to record themselves during practice sessions. Listening to recordings helps identify areas for improvement and provides a different perspective on their playing. Self-evaluation promotes critical listening and enhances self-awareness.

12. Consistent Schedule:

- Establish a consistent practice schedule tailored to the child's age and attention span. Shorter, focused practice sessions are more effective than infrequent, lengthy ones. Consistency develops discipline and ensures steady progress.

13. Review Previously Learned Material:

- Allocate time to review previously learned pieces or exercises. This maintains repertoire and reinforces technical skills. It also helps develop a solid foundation for advanced repertoire.

14. Seek Guidance:

- Encourage the child to seek guidance from their teacher or mentor. Regular lessons provide feedback, corrections, and new insights. A qualified instructor can offer guidance on practice techniques and help set realistic goals.

15. Celebrate Achievements:

- Acknowledge and celebrate achievements along the way. Recognize progress, no matter how small, to boost motivation and instill a positive attitude towards practice.

Creating effective practice routines involves a balance between technique, musicality, and personal growth. By incorporating these techniques and establishing structured practice sessions, young violinists can develop discipline, improve technical proficiency, and nurture a lifelong love for music.

SETTING GOALS AND PRIORITIZING PRACTICE AREAS

Setting goals and prioritizing practice areas are essential for children violinists to focus their efforts, track progress, and achieve meaningful growth in their musical journey. By establishing clear objectives and identifying areas that require attention, young violinists can optimize their practice sessions and make the most of their practice time. Here is an extensive guide on setting goals and prioritizing practice areas for children violinists:

1. Assess Current Skills:

- Begin by assessing the child's current skills and abilities on the violin. Evaluate their technical proficiency, intonation, bowing technique, rhythm, sight-reading ability, and musicality. This assessment serves as a baseline to identify areas for improvement.

2. Establish Long-Term Goals:

- Collaborate with the child to establish long-term goals. These goals can be specific, such as learning a particular piece, participating in a competition, or advancing to a higher level. Long-term goals provide a sense of direction and purpose.

3. Break Down Goals:

 - Break down long-term goals into smaller, manageable objectives. Divide them into short-term goals that can be achieved within a few weeks or months. Breaking down goals makes them more attainable and facilitates progress tracking.

4. Prioritize Areas of Improvement:

 - Identify specific areas of improvement based on the child's assessment and long-term goals. Prioritize the areas that require the most attention and focus. This could include intonation, bow control, rhythm, sight-reading, or specific technical challenges.

5. Set Specific Practice Targets:

- Set specific practice targets related to the prioritized areas of improvement. For example, if intonation is a priority, the target could be to practice scales or exercises that specifically address intonation for a certain amount of time each day.

6. Allocate Practice Time:

- Allocate dedicated practice time for each prioritized area. Divide practice sessions into segments, devoting a specific amount of time to each area of focus. This ensures that all areas receive attention and progress is made across multiple aspects of violin playing.

7. Establish Practice Routine:

  - Establish a consistent practice routine that incorporates the prioritized areas. Determine the order in which the areas will be practiced, considering the child's energy levels and attention span. Consistency in practice routines promotes discipline and steady progress.

8. Practice with Purpose:

  - Encourage the child to practice with purpose and focus. Each practice session should have a specific objective or target, whether it's improving intonation, mastering a technical passage, or refining a particular musical phrase. Practice with intention enhances efficiency and results.

230

9. Monitor Progress:

- Regularly monitor and evaluate the child's progress towards their goals. Keep track of achievements, milestones, and areas that still need improvement. This feedback loop enables adjustments to practice strategies and provides motivation through visible progress.

10. Seek Guidance:

- Encourage the child to seek guidance from their teacher or mentor in setting goals and prioritizing practice areas. Experienced instructors can provide valuable insights, offer tailored exercises, and help refine practice routines based on the child's needs and aspirations.

231

11. Celebrate Milestones:

- Celebrate milestones and achievements along the way. Acknowledge the child's progress, no matter how small, to boost motivation and foster a positive attitude towards practice. Celebrations can be as simple as verbal praise or small rewards.

12. Adjust Goals as Needed:

- Be flexible in adjusting goals as the child progresses. As certain areas of focus improve, reassess and set new goals that align with their advancing skills. This ensures continuous growth and avoids stagnation.

13. Emphasize Balance:

- Emphasize a balanced approach to practicing. While it's important to address areas that need improvement, incorporate time for enjoyable repertoire or creative exploration. Balancing technical development with musical expression sustains motivation and enthusiasm.

14. Reflect and Evaluate:

- Encourage the child to reflect on their practice sessions and evaluate their own progress. Foster self-awareness by asking questions such as, "What went well today?" and "What could be improved?" Self-reflection cultivates a sense of ownership and accountability.

15. *Foster a Love for Music:*

  - Above all, foster a love for music and the joy of playing the violin. Encourage the child to explore different musical styles, listen to recordings, attend live performances, and engage with other musicians. Nurturing a passion for music fuels intrinsic motivation and sustains long-term dedication.

By setting goals, prioritizing practice areas, and maintaining a balanced approach, children violinists can effectively focus their efforts and make meaningful progress in their musical development. This intentional approach to practice fosters discipline, self-reflection, and a lifelong love for playing the violin.

BREAKING DOWN DIFFICULT PASSAGES

Breaking down difficult passages into manageable parts is a valuable technique for children violinists to tackle challenging music effectively. By approaching complex sections systematically, young violinists can build confidence, improve accuracy, and overcome technical hurdles. Here is an extensive guide on breaking down difficult passages for children violinists:

1. Identify the Difficult Passage:

- Start by identifying the specific section or passage that poses a challenge. It could be a fast passage, complex rhythms, intricate bowing patterns, or demanding fingerings. Pinpointing the exact difficulty helps in devising a targeted practice strategy.

2. Analyze the Passage:

- Carefully analyze the passage to understand its musical and technical elements. Identify patterns, intervals, fingerings, and bowings involved. Pay attention to dynamics, articulations, and phrasing indications as they impact interpretation and execution.

3. Isolate Problematic Measures:

- Break down the passage into smaller, manageable units. Identify the measures or bars that are particularly challenging. Isolate these measures to

237

focus on them individually, ensuring a thorough understanding and mastery.

4. Practice Slowly:

- Begin practicing the isolated measures at a slow tempo. Slow practice allows for careful attention to detail, precision, and accuracy. Practice with a metronome, gradually increasing the tempo as proficiency improves.

5. Focus on Fingerings:

- Pay close attention to fingerings in the difficult passage. Evaluate and experiment with different fingerings to find the most efficient and comfortable options. Ensure that fingerings facilitate smooth shifts, accurate intonation, and ease of execution.

6. Bowing Techniques:

   - Address bowing techniques specific to the passage. Determine the appropriate bow division, bow direction (up-bow or down-bow), and bowing styles (legato, staccato, spiccato, etc.). Experiment with different bowing variations to achieve the desired musical expression.

7. Practice in Short Sections:

   - Divide the difficult passage into shorter sections, working on two to four measures at a time. Focus on these sections individually until they are mastered. Once proficient,

239

gradually connect the sections to reconstruct the complete passage.

8. Repetition and Muscle Memory:

- Emphasize repetition to develop muscle memory. Repeat the isolated sections multiple times, ensuring consistent fingerings, bowings, and musical expression. Repetition strengthens neural connections, automates challenging movements, and improves overall fluency.

9. Use Different Practice Techniques:

- Incorporate various practice techniques to address specific challenges within the passage. This may include rhythmic variations, accenting different beats, practicing in different dynamics, or experimenting with different articulations. These techniques enhance control and understanding of the passage.

10. Slowly Increase Tempo:

- Gradually increase the tempo as proficiency improves. Practice with a metronome, adding a few beats per minute at a time. Maintain accuracy and control at each tempo before advancing further. This gradual tempo increase builds confidence and solidifies muscle memory.

11. Practice Transitions:

- Pay special attention to the transitions between difficult measures

241

or sections. Isolate these transition points and practice them separately. Smooth out any technical or musical challenges encountered during the transitions for a seamless performance.

12. Record and Evaluate:

- Record practice sessions to evaluate progress and identify areas that need further refinement. Listening to recordings provides an objective perspective and helps pinpoint areas for improvement. Self-evaluation fosters critical listening skills and guides targeted practice.

13. Seek Guidance:

- Seek guidance from a teacher or mentor when encountering persistent difficulties. Experienced instructors can provide insights, offer specific exercises, or suggest alternative approaches to overcome technical challenges. Their expertise and feedback are invaluable resources.

14. Practice with Musical Context:

- Once the difficult passage is mastered in isolation, reintegrate it into the larger musical context. Practice playing the passage within the surrounding phrases and sections to ensure seamless integration and musical continuity.

243

15. *Celebrate Achievements:*

   - Celebrate milestones and achievements as the child makes progress in mastering the difficult passage. Recognize their efforts and perseverance, reinforcing a positive attitude towards tackling challenges. Celebrations can range from verbal praise to small rewards.

By breaking down difficult passages into manageable parts and employing focused practice techniques, children violinists can overcome technical obstacles and master challenging music. This systematic approach builds confidence, enhances technical proficiency, and paves the way for artistic expression and musical growth.

BUILDING STAMINA AND ENDURANCE

Developing stamina and endurance is crucial for children violinists to sustain long practice sessions, perform challenging repertoire, and enhance overall playing abilities. By implementing effective strategies, young violinists can gradually build their physical and mental stamina, improving their endurance for extended periods of playing. Here is an extensive guide on building stamina and endurance for children violinists:

1. Gradual Increase in Practice Time:

  - Begin by gradually increasing practice time over a period of weeks or months. Start with shorter practice sessions and gradually extend the duration as the child's stamina improves. This gradual approach prevents overexertion and allows the body to adapt.

2. Consistent Practice Schedule:

- Establish a consistent practice schedule and stick to it. Regular practice sessions help the body and mind adapt to the demands of playing the violin. Consistency builds endurance over time and establishes a disciplined practice routine.

3. Proper Warm-up:

- Prior to practice, ensure the child engages in a thorough warm-up

246

routine. This can include gentle stretching exercises, finger exercises, and bowing exercises to warm up the muscles and prepare them for extended playing.

4. Posture and Ergonomics:

- Emphasize proper posture and ergonomics while playing the violin. Correct body alignment and positioning reduce tension and fatigue, allowing for longer playing sessions. Encourage the child to maintain a relaxed and balanced posture throughout practice.

5. Incremental Repertoire Difficulty:

- Gradually introduce increasingly challenging repertoire to build

247

endurance. Start with simpler pieces and gradually progress to more complex compositions. This progressive approach helps the child adapt to the physical and mental demands of playing difficult music.

6. Focus on Technique:

- Place emphasis on developing solid technique. A strong technical foundation increases efficiency and reduces physical strain. Focus on proper hand position, bowing technique, shifting, and intonation. A sound technique reduces unnecessary tension and conserves energy.

7. Interval Training:

- Incorporate interval training during practice sessions. Alternate between periods of intense, focused practice and short breaks for rest and recovery. This interval training approach gradually builds endurance by challenging the body and allowing for adequate rest.

8. Targeted Exercises:

  - Include targeted exercises in practice sessions to build specific muscle groups used in violin playing. This can include finger exercises, bowing exercises, scales, arpeggios, and double-stop exercises. These exercises strengthen the muscles and improve stamina.

9. Gradual Tempo Increase:

- When working on challenging passages or pieces, gradually increase the tempo over time. Start at a comfortable tempo and gradually push the boundaries by incrementally increasing the speed. This progressive tempo increase builds stamina and accuracy.

10. Focus on Breath Control:

- Encourage the child to focus on breath control while playing. Deep, relaxed breathing supplies oxygen to the muscles, reducing tension and enhancing endurance. Remind them to take deep breaths at appropriate moments, such as during rests or longer sustained notes.

11. Mental Focus and Concentration:

- Develop mental focus and concentration during practice. Help the child stay engaged and attentive throughout the entire practice session. Mental stamina is just as important as physical stamina, and cultivating focus enhances overall endurance.

12. Cross-Training Activities:

- Engage in cross-training activities to build overall physical fitness. Encourage the child to participate in activities such as swimming, cycling, or yoga that improve cardiovascular fitness, flexibility, and core strength. A well-rounded fitness regimen supports violin playing endurance.

251

13. Gradual Increase in Repetitions:

- Gradually increase the number of repetitions for challenging passages or exercises. Start with a manageable number and gradually add more repetitions over time. This progressive increase builds endurance and strengthens the muscles involved.

14. Rest and Recovery:

- Ensure the child gets adequate rest and recovery between practice sessions. Allow for regular breaks during practice, and ensure they have sufficient sleep and downtime to rejuvenate the body and mind. Proper rest promotes physical and mental endurance.

15. *Positive Mindset and Motivation:*

- Foster a positive mindset and motivation in the child. Encourage them to set goals, celebrate milestones, and maintain a positive attitude towards building endurance. A motivated and optimistic approach helps overcome challenges and sustain long-term progress.

By implementing these strategies, children violinists can gradually build stamina and endurance, enabling them to tackle challenging repertoire, sustain longer practice sessions, and perform with confidence. The combination of physical conditioning, mental focus, and a disciplined approach lays the foundation for continued growth and enjoyment in violin playing.

253

OVERCOMING CHALLENGES AND FRUSTRATIONS IN VIOLIN PRACTICE

Learning the violin can present various challenges and frustrations for children violinists. It is essential to help them navigate these obstacles and develop strategies to overcome difficulties effectively. By fostering a positive mindset, providing support, and implementing effective practice techniques, children can tackle challenges head-on and experience growth in their violin playing. Here is an extensive guide on overcoming challenges and frustrations in violin practice for children violinists:

1. Set Realistic Expectations:

  - Help children set realistic expectations about their progress. Encourage them to focus on personal growth rather than comparing themselves to others. Remind them that learning the violin is a journey, and progress takes time and dedication.

2. Break Down Challenges:

  - Break down challenging passages or techniques into smaller, manageable parts. Focus on one specific difficulty at a time and work on it until it improves. By tackling challenges in smaller increments, children can build confidence and gradually overcome frustrations.

3. Practice Mindfully:

   - Encourage children to practice mindfully, focusing on each note, bowing, and technique. Mindful practice promotes concentration and attention to detail, helping them address specific challenges effectively.

4. Seek Guidance:

   - Encourage children to seek guidance from their violin teacher or mentor when facing persistent challenges. Experienced instructors can provide valuable insights, offer targeted exercises, and suggest alternative approaches to overcome specific difficulties.

5. Patience and Perseverance:

- Teach children the value of patience and perseverance. Remind them that progress may not always be immediate, but with consistent effort, they can overcome challenges and achieve their goals.

6. Positive Reinforcement:

- Provide positive reinforcement and encouragement during practice sessions. Celebrate small victories and milestones, emphasizing the child's progress and effort. Positive reinforcement boosts motivation and confidence, helping children overcome frustration.

7. Practice in Different Ways:

  - Vary the practice routine to keep children engaged and motivated. Incorporate fun and creative practice techniques, such as playing along with recordings, using music apps or games, or performing for family and friends. These alternative approaches can alleviate frustration and bring joy to the learning process.

8. Focus on Strengths:

  - Identify and focus on the child's strengths as a violinist. By acknowledging and nurturing their natural abilities, they will gain confidence and develop a positive self-image, which can help counteract frustrations.

259

9. Analyze Mistakes Constructively:

   - Encourage children to view mistakes as learning opportunities rather than failures. Help them analyze mistakes constructively, understanding the underlying causes and developing strategies to correct them. Mistakes are stepping stones to improvement.

10. Take Breaks:

   - If frustration builds up during practice, encourage children to take short breaks. Stepping away from the violin for a few minutes can help clear the mind and alleviate frustration. Remind them that breaks are part of the learning process and can enhance productivity.

260

11. Visualize Success:

   - Teach children to visualize success and imagine themselves overcoming challenges. Visualization techniques can help them develop a positive mindset, build confidence, and overcome frustrations.

12. Learn from Role Models:

   - Expose children to inspiring performances and stories of accomplished violinists. Learning about the challenges these musicians faced and how they overcame them can inspire and motivate children to persist in their own practice.

13. Emphasize the Joy of Music:

- Remind children of the joy and beauty of music. Encourage them to connect emotionally with the music they play, focusing on the expressive and artistic aspects of violin playing. Cultivating a love for music can help them overcome frustrations and stay motivated.

14. Record Progress:

- Encourage children to record their practice sessions and performances. Regularly reviewing these recordings allows them to track their progress over time, providing tangible evidence of improvement and helping them stay motivated.

262

15. *Cultivate a Supportive Environment:*

- Create a supportive practice environment for children. Offer encouragement, patience, and understanding. Let them know that mistakes and challenges are normal parts of the learning process, and that you are there to support them every step of the way.

By implementing these strategies, children violinists can develop resilience, overcome challenges, and manage frustration during their violin practice. With patience, perseverance, and a positive mindset, they will experience growth, progress, and a deepening love for the violin.

DEALING WITH MISTAKES AND PERFORMANCE ANXIETY

Mistakes and performance anxiety are common challenges that children violinists may encounter during their musical journey. Learning to cope with these difficulties is crucial for their growth and development as performers. By adopting effective strategies, children can navigate mistakes and performance anxiety in a healthy and productive manner. Here is an extensive guide on dealing with mistakes and performance anxiety for children violinists:

1. Normalize Mistakes:

- Help children understand that making mistakes is a natural part of the learning process. Emphasize that even professional musicians make mistakes. By normalizing mistakes, children can develop a healthier attitude towards them and view them as opportunities for growth.

2. Reframe Mistakes as Learning Opportunities:

- Encourage children to reframe mistakes as valuable learning opportunities. Teach them to analyze their mistakes objectively, identify the underlying causes, and develop strategies to correct them. By embracing mistakes, children can turn them into stepping stones for improvement.

3. Break Down Mistakes:

   - When a mistake occurs, guide children to break it down and analyze its components. Identify the specific technique or musical element that needs improvement and work on it separately. Breaking down mistakes into manageable parts makes them less overwhelming and easier to address.

4. Practice Problem-Solving:

   - Teach children problem-solving skills to tackle mistakes effectively. Encourage them to experiment with different approaches, techniques, or practice methods to overcome specific challenges. Developing problem-solving skills empowers children to take control of their learning process.

266

5. Positive Self-Talk:

 - Teach children to use positive self-talk to counter negative thoughts and emotions associated with mistakes. Encourage them to replace self-criticism with self-compassion and constructive feedback. Positive self-talk builds resilience and fosters a healthy mindset.

6. Incremental Repetition:

 - Address mistakes through incremental repetition. Break down challenging sections and practice them slowly and accurately. Gradually increase the tempo as the child gains confidence and proficiency. Incremental repetition helps build

267

muscle memory and reduces the likelihood of repeating mistakes.

7. Learn from Successful Performances:

- Remind children of successful performances they have had in the past. Encourage them to recall the positive experiences, the joy they felt, and the applause they received. Reflecting on past successes instills confidence and reminds them of their capabilities.

8. Visualization Techniques:

- Introduce visualization techniques to help children manage performance anxiety. Encourage them to visualize themselves performing confidently and

268

successfully. Visualization helps reduce anxiety, enhances focus, and reinforces positive performance outcomes.

9. Controlled Breathing Exercises:

   - Teach children controlled breathing exercises to manage performance anxiety. Deep, diaphragmatic breathing triggers the body's relaxation response, reducing the physical symptoms of anxiety and promoting a sense of calmness and control.

10. Performance Opportunities:

   - Provide children with regular performance opportunities in a supportive environment. This can include playing for family and friends,

269

participating in recitals, or joining youth orchestras or chamber groups. Frequent performances help children become more comfortable on stage, gradually reducing performance anxiety.

11. Mock Performances and Simulations:

- Conduct mock performances or simulations at home or in a familiar setting. Create an environment similar to an actual performance and have the child play through their repertoire. This helps them become accustomed to the pressure and expectations of a live performance.

12. Focus on the Process, Not Just the Outcome:

- Shift the focus from solely emphasizing the outcome of a performance to valuing the process of learning and growth. Help children understand that mistakes and setbacks are part of the journey and that their progress as musicians goes beyond a single performance.

13. Supportive Practice Environment:

- Foster a supportive practice environment where mistakes are viewed as opportunities for improvement, rather than sources of frustration or disappointment. Encourage open communication, patience, and understanding. This

271

creates a safe space for children to explore and learn without fear of judgment.

14. Gratitude and Reflection:

- Encourage children to reflect on their progress and express gratitude for their musical journey. Help them recognize the effort they put into their practice and acknowledge the joy and fulfillment that music brings to their lives. Gratitude fosters a positive mindset and reduces anxiety.

15. Professional Guidance:

- If performance anxiety persists or becomes significantly challenging, consider seeking professional guidance from a qualified music teacher or a mental health professional specializing in performance anxiety. They can provide tailored strategies and support to help children overcome their specific challenges.

By implementing these strategies, children violinists can develop resilience, manage mistakes effectively, and navigate performance anxiety. They will build confidence, enjoy their musical journey, and thrive as performers. Remember to create a supportive and nurturing environment that encourages growth and celebrates the joy of music.

SEEKING GUIDANCE AND SUPPORT

For children violinists, seeking guidance and support is crucial for their musical development and overall growth as musicians. Whether it's assistance from experienced teachers, collaboration with peers, or the support of family and friends, having a strong support system can greatly enhance a child's violin journey. Here is an extensive guide on seeking guidance and support for children violinists:

1. Experienced Violin Teachers:

- Enroll your child in violin lessons with an experienced and qualified teacher. A knowledgeable instructor can provide valuable guidance, personalized instruction, and feedback tailored to the child's skill level and goals. The teacher will help develop proper technique, musicality, and address specific challenges.

2. Mentorship Programs:

- Explore mentorship programs for children violinists. These programs connect young musicians with accomplished violinists who can serve as role models and provide guidance based on their own experiences. Mentors can offer insights, share practice strategies, and provide inspiration for the child's musical journey.

3. Music Schools and Conservatories:

- Consider enrolling your child in a reputable music school or conservatory that offers specialized programs for young violinists. These institutions often have faculty members who are dedicated to nurturing young talent and providing comprehensive musical education.

4. Workshops and Masterclasses:

- Encourage your child to participate in workshops and masterclasses led by renowned violinists. These events offer opportunities for children to receive guidance and feedback from experts in the field. They can learn from different perspectives, gain new insights, and refine their skills.

276

5. Orchestra and Ensemble Participation:

   - Encourage your child to join a youth orchestra or ensemble. Collaborating with peers who share a passion for music provides a supportive and motivating environment. Playing in a group setting enhances ensemble skills, fosters teamwork, and offers opportunities for musical growth through shared experiences.

6. Music Camps and Festivals:

   - Explore music camps and festivals that cater to young violinists. These programs often feature intensive workshops, rehearsals, and performances, allowing children to

277

immerse themselves in a musical community and receive guidance from professional musicians and educators.

7. Parental Involvement:

- Parents can play a significant role in providing guidance and support for their child's violin journey. Attend lessons and recitals, engage in regular communication with the teacher, and assist with practice routines. By being actively involved, parents can reinforce the importance of music and provide emotional support to their child.

8. Online Resources and Communities:

- Utilize online resources and communities dedicated to supporting

278

young violinists. Websites, forums, and social media groups provide a platform for sharing experiences, seeking advice, and connecting with other parents, teachers, and students. Online platforms can supplement traditional guidance and support systems.

9. Peer Support:

   - Encourage your child to connect with other young violinists and form peer support networks. This can be achieved through participation in group classes, chamber music ensembles, or attending music camps. Peer support fosters a sense of camaraderie, provides motivation, and encourages shared learning experiences.

10. Recording and Self-Evaluation:

- Encourage your child to record their practice sessions and performances. This allows them to evaluate their progress objectively and identify areas for improvement. Self-evaluation helps children become more self-aware and proactive in seeking guidance for specific challenges.

11. Performance Opportunities:

- Seek out performance opportunities for your child, such as recitals, community concerts, or school events. Regularly performing in front of an audience builds confidence, provides valuable experience, and offers opportunities for feedback and support from teachers, peers, and audiences.

12. Music Education Organizations:

   - Explore music education organizations that offer resources, workshops, and programs for young musicians. These organizations often provide scholarships, grants, and mentorship opportunities. They can connect your child to a broader network of musicians and educators.

13. Emotional Support:

   - Provide emotional support to your child throughout their violin journey. Encourage them during challenging times, celebrate their accomplishments, and be understanding of their frustrations. Emotional support fosters a positive

281

mindset, resilience, and a love for
music.

14. Communication with Teachers:

   - Maintain open lines of
communication with your child's violin
teacher. Regularly discuss their
progress, challenges, and goals.
Collaborate with the teacher to develop
a personalized practice plan and
address any concerns or questions.
Communication ensures that everyone
is working together to support the
child's musical development.

15. Celebrate Milestones:

   - Celebrate your child's milestones,
both big and small. Recognize their
achievements, whether it's successfully

learning a new piece, performing in a recital, or receiving positive feedback. Celebrating milestones reinforces their progress, boosts confidence, and motivates them to continue seeking guidance and support.

By actively seeking guidance and support for your child, you create an environment that nurtures their musical growth and fosters their love for the violin. Remember to be proactive, explore various resources and opportunities, and maintain open communication with teachers, mentors, and fellow musicians. With the support of a strong network, your child can thrive as a violinist and enjoy a fulfilling musical journey.

CONCLUSION: THE JOURNEY OF LEARNING

The journey of learning the violin for children is an exciting and transformative experience. It is a path filled with challenges, growth, and immense joy. Throughout this journey, children violinists embark on a remarkable musical adventure that shapes their character, discipline, and artistic expression. As they navigate the intricacies of learning an instrument, they acquire valuable skills that extend far beyond the realm of music.

The journey of learning the violin instills in children a sense of dedication and perseverance. They learn firsthand the importance of consistent practice,

284

patience, and resilience. Through countless hours spent refining techniques, tackling difficult passages, and striving for musicality, children develop a strong work ethic and a deep understanding of the rewards that come from persistent effort.

Alongside technical proficiency, children violinists also cultivate their creativity and expression. They learn to interpret musical compositions, infuse their own emotions into the music, and communicate their unique voice through the instrument. The violin becomes an extension of their own identity, allowing them to express themselves in a profoundly personal and artistic way.

The journey of learning the violin is not without its challenges. Children encounter obstacles, make mistakes, and experience moments of frustration. However, these challenges serve as opportunities for growth and self-discovery. Each mistake becomes a stepping stone towards improvement, and every hurdle they overcome builds their confidence and resilience.

Support and guidance play a vital role in the journey of a young violinist. Experienced teachers, mentors, peers, and family provide the necessary encouragement, knowledge, and emotional support. They help children navigate technical difficulties, offer guidance in musical interpretation, and provide a nurturing environment that fosters their love for music.

As children progress in their violin journey, they are exposed to various performance opportunities. Recitals, competitions, and ensemble performances allow them to showcase their hard work and share their musical talents with others. These experiences not only build their stage presence and confidence but also cultivate a sense of community and collaboration with fellow musicians.

The journey of learning the violin is not solely about reaching a destination but about embracing the process. It is about fostering a deep appreciation for music, nurturing a lifelong love for learning, and developing a profound connection with the instrument. The journey teaches children the value of

287

discipline, self-expression, teamwork, and the ability to overcome challenges.

Ultimately, the journey of learning the violin for children is a transformative and rewarding experience. It shapes their character, hones their skills, and opens a world of artistic possibilities. As children navigate this musical voyage, they not only become skilled violinists but also grow into well-rounded individuals with a profound appreciation for music and a passion that will accompany them throughout their lives.

Made in United States
Troutdale, OR
10/24/2024

24107450R00166